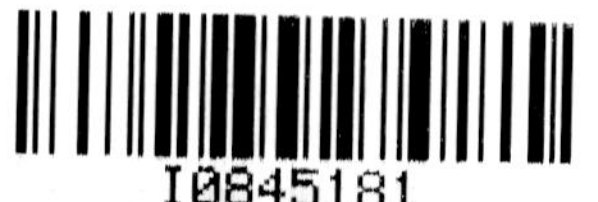

THE GOOD BOY COLORING BOOK

This book belongs to:

____

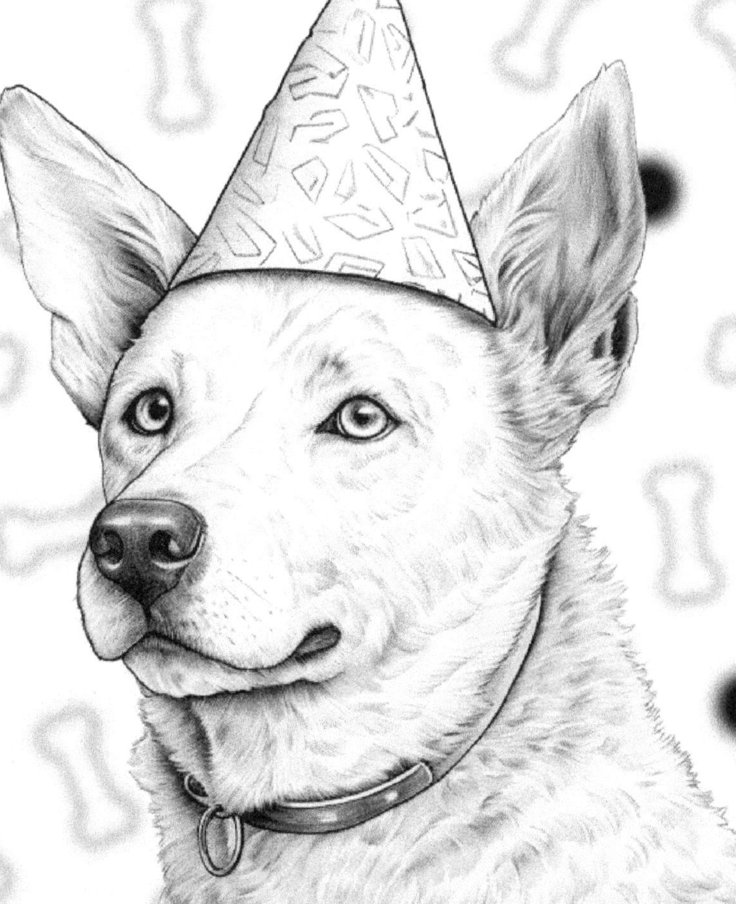

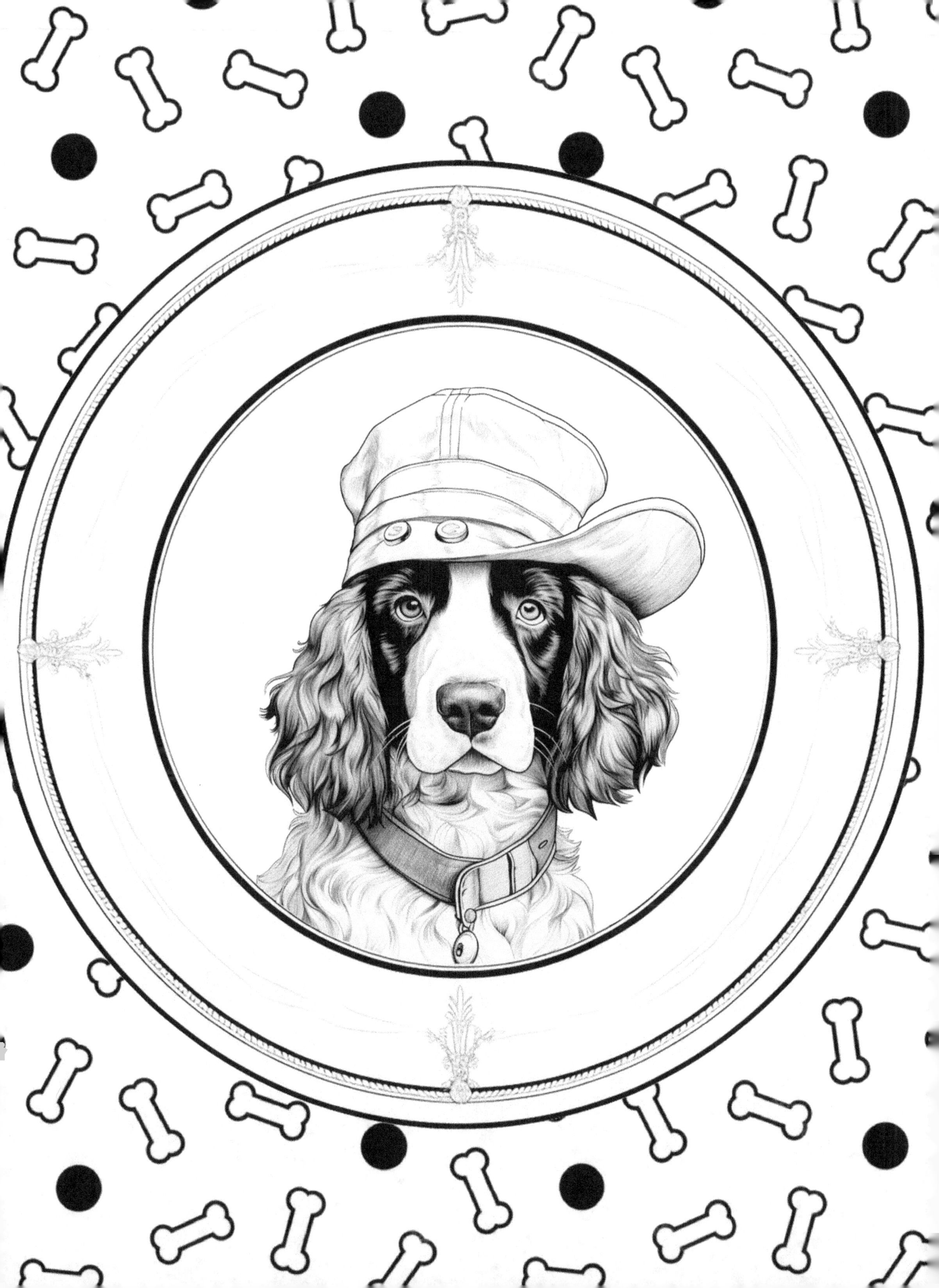

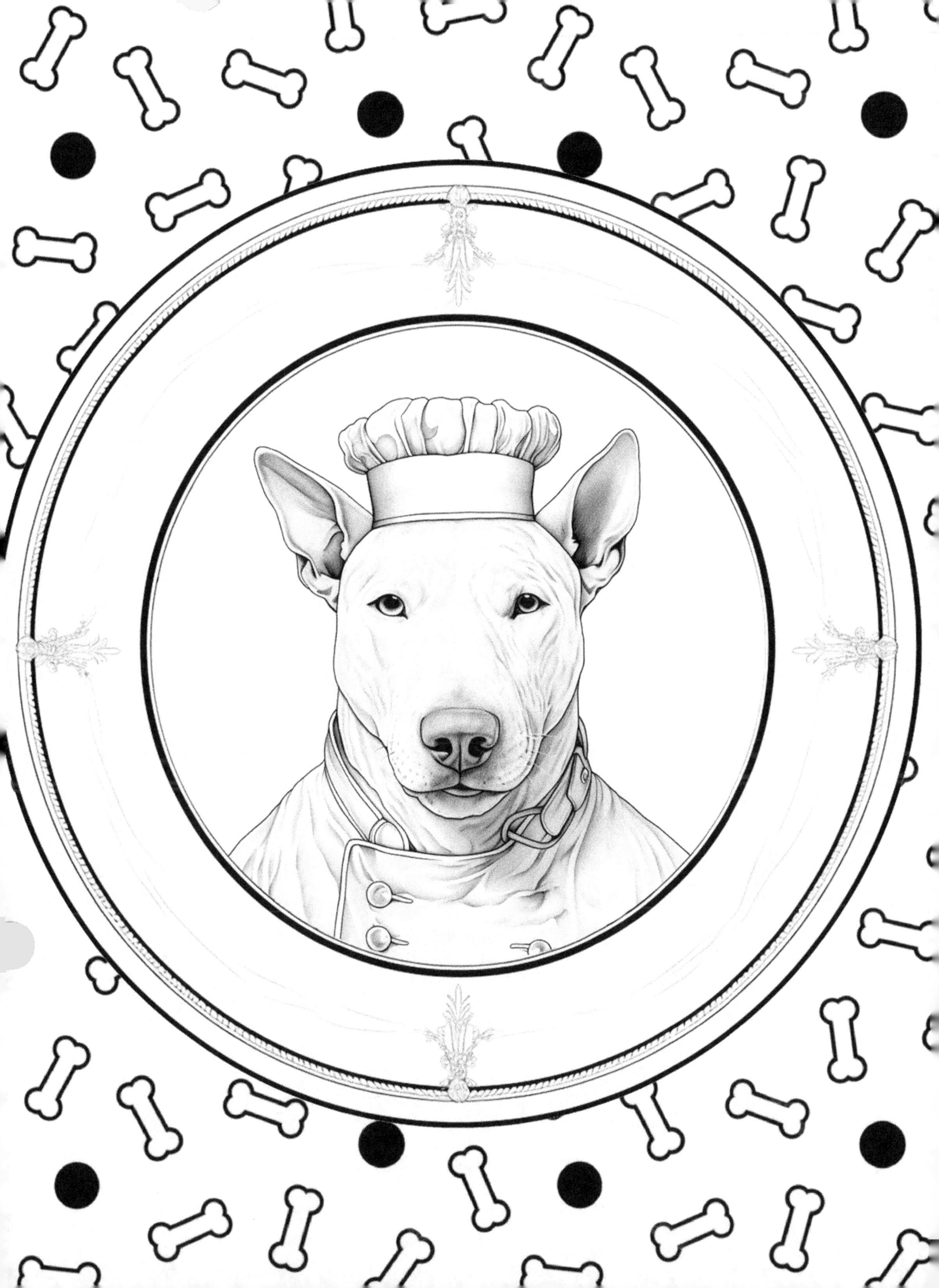

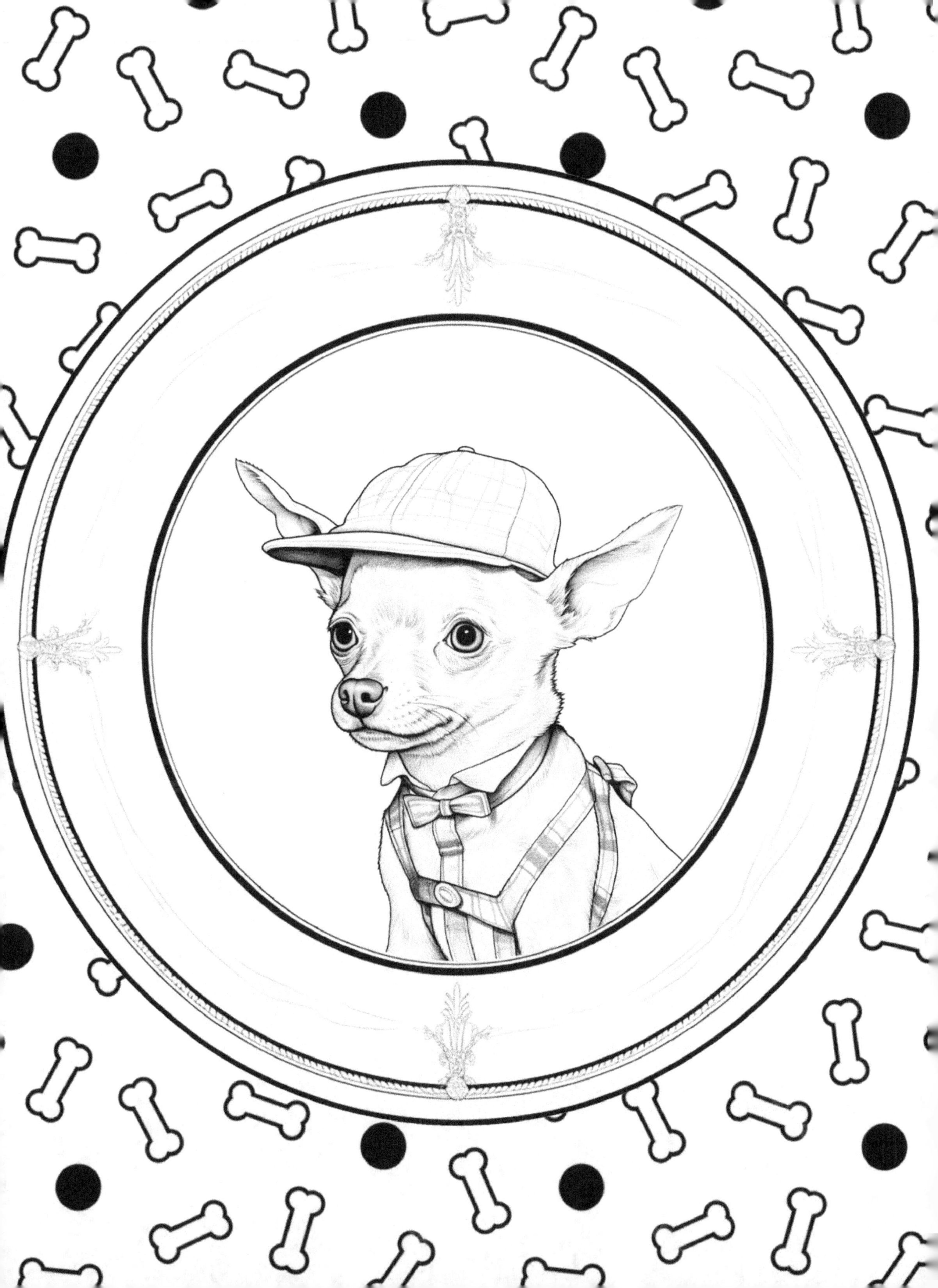

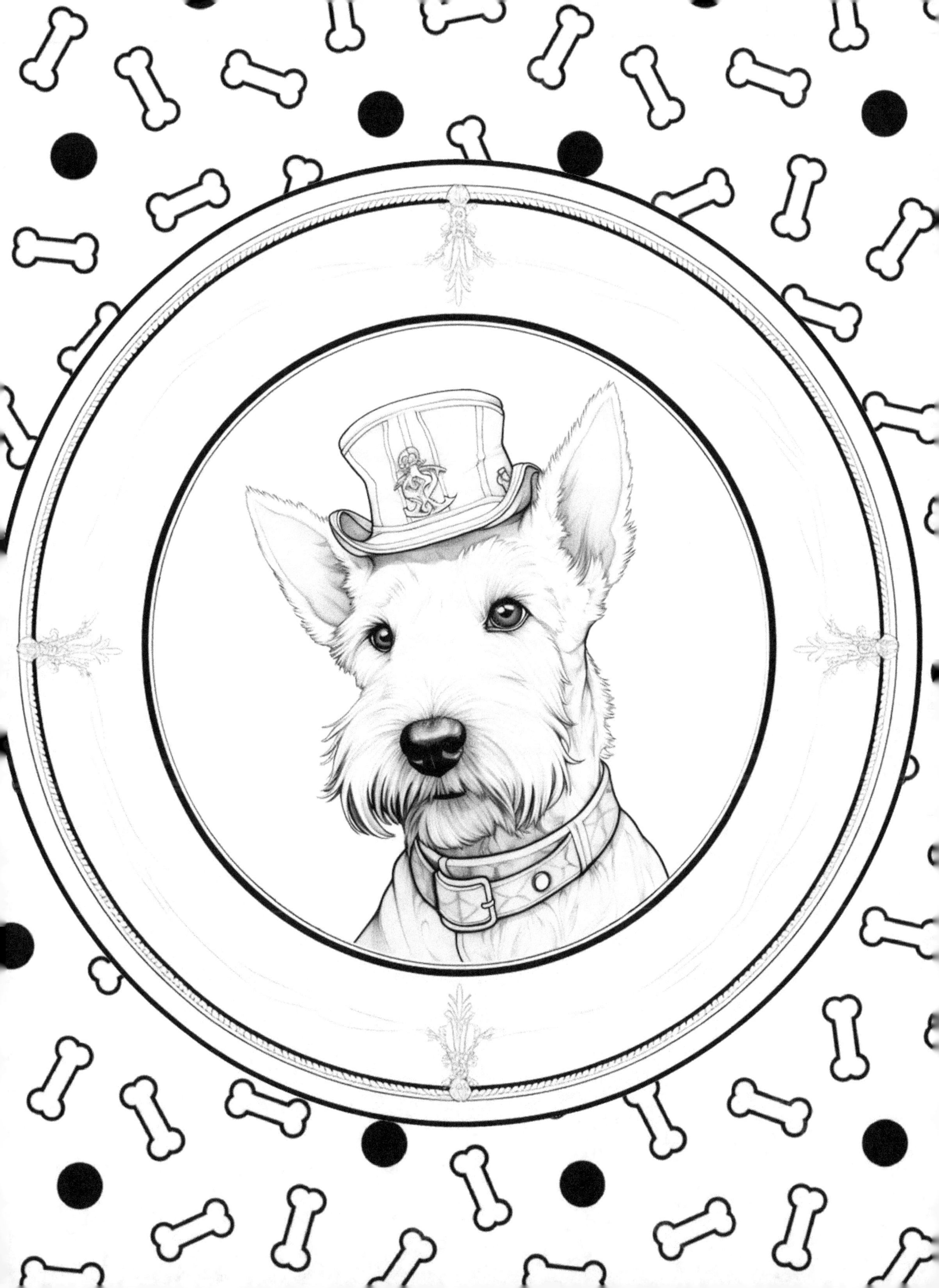

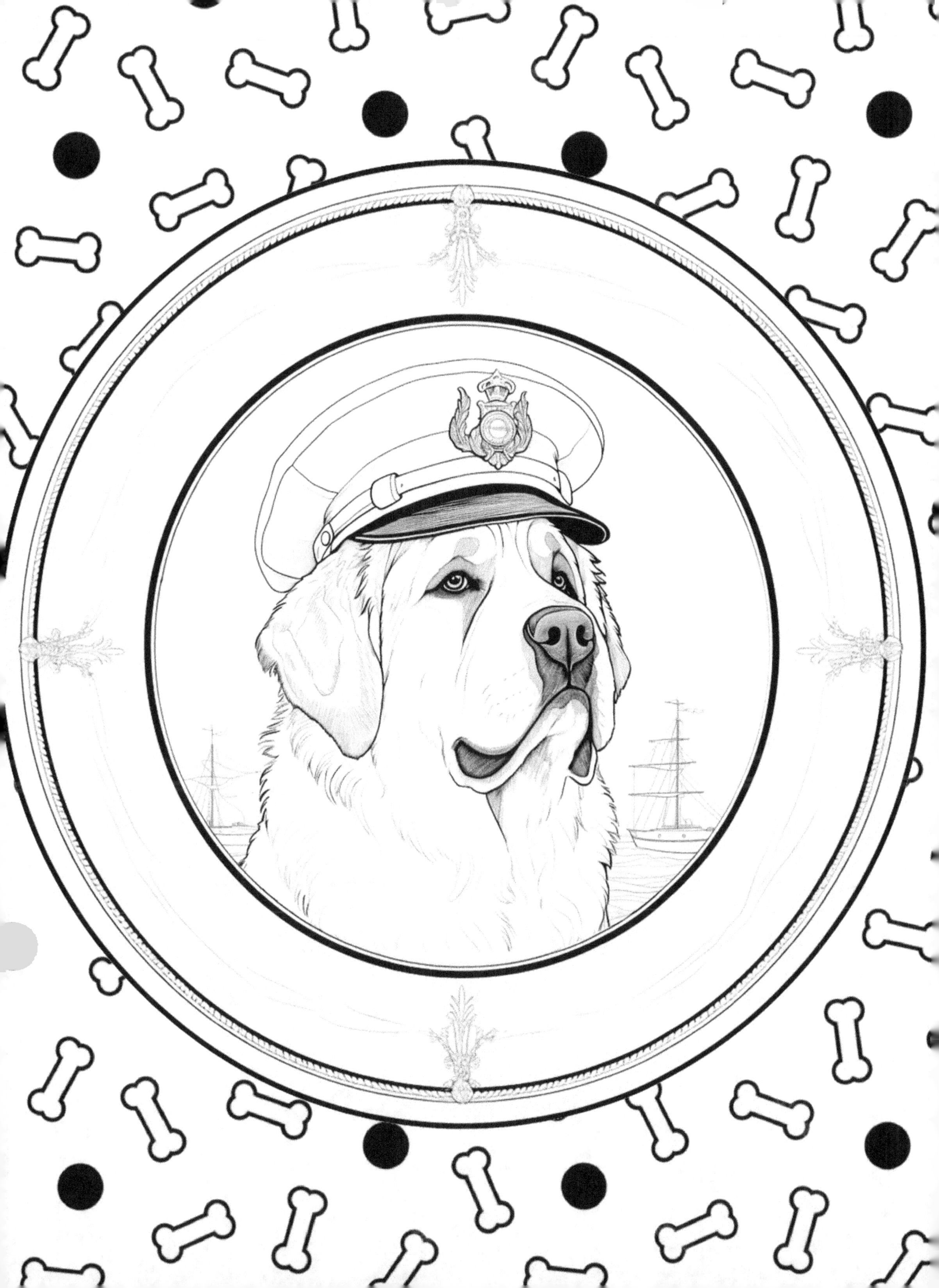

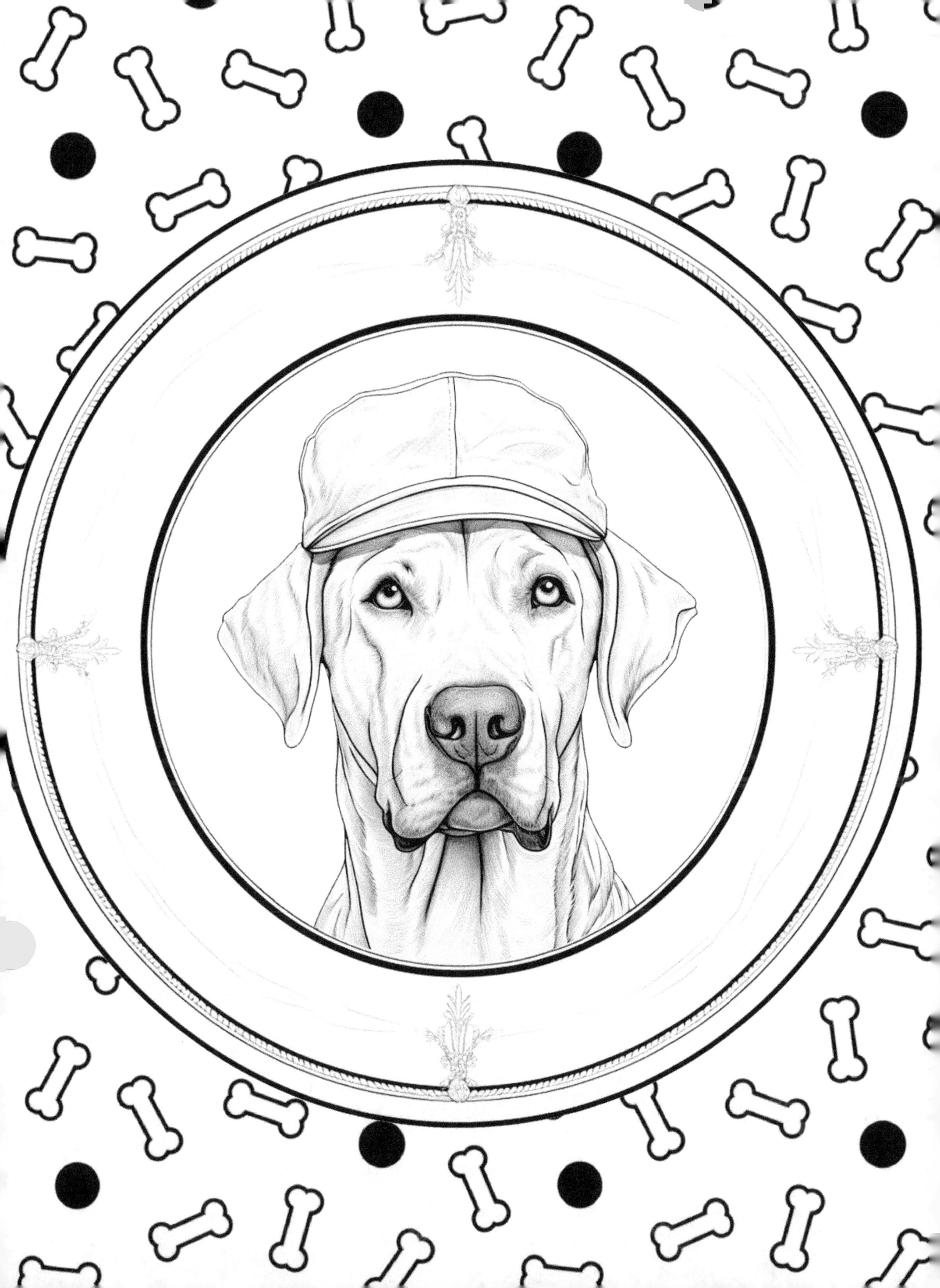

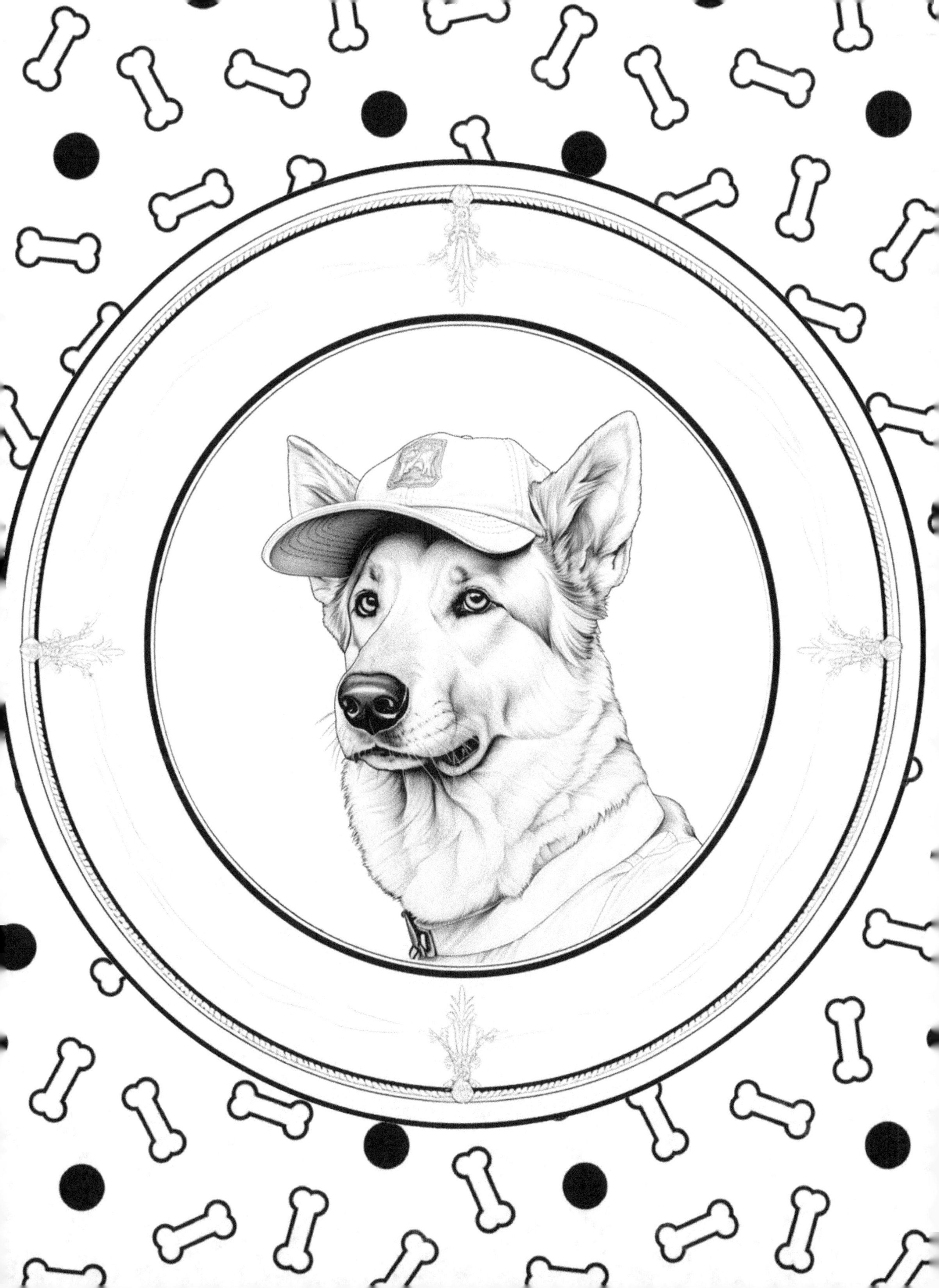

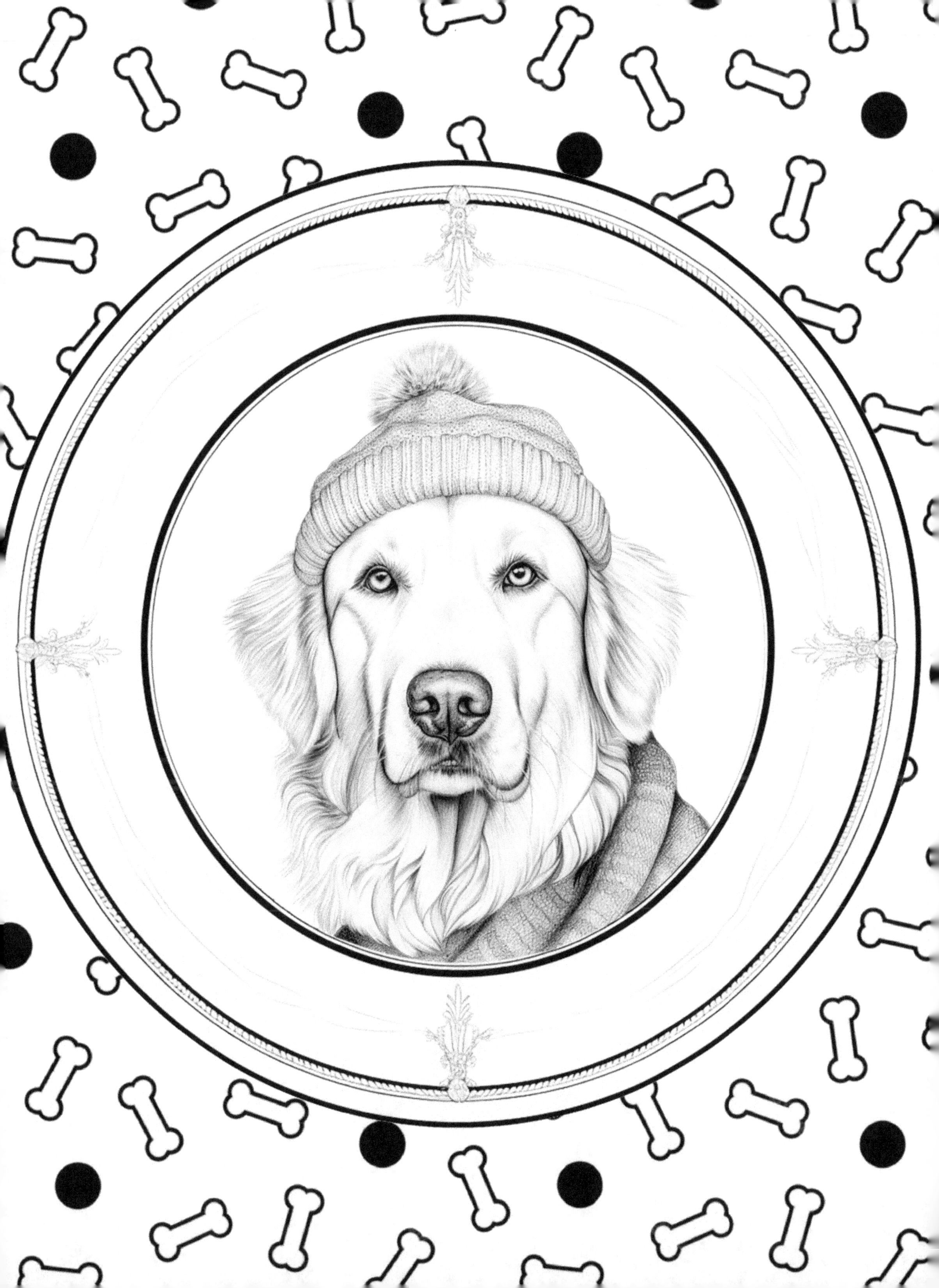

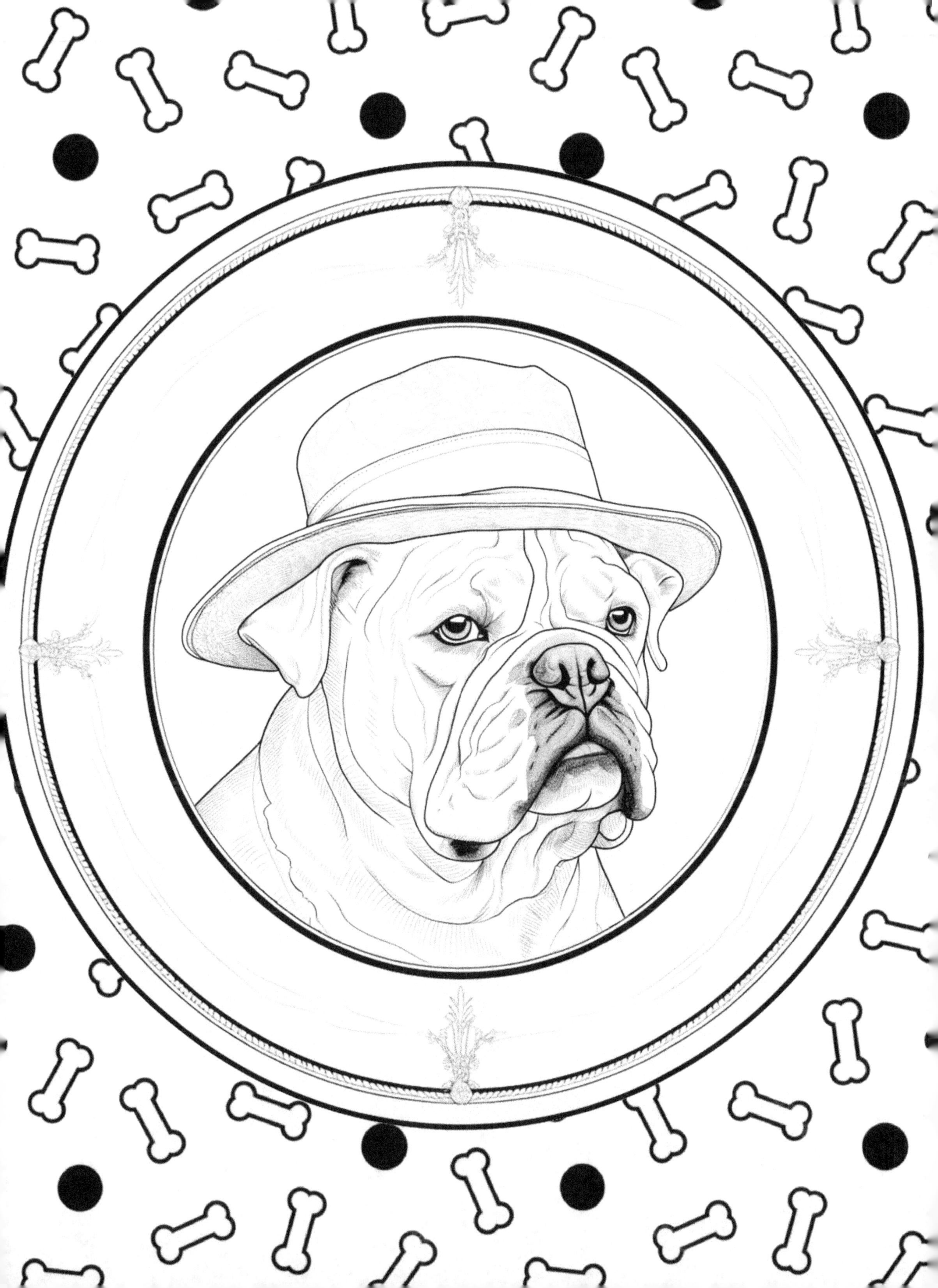

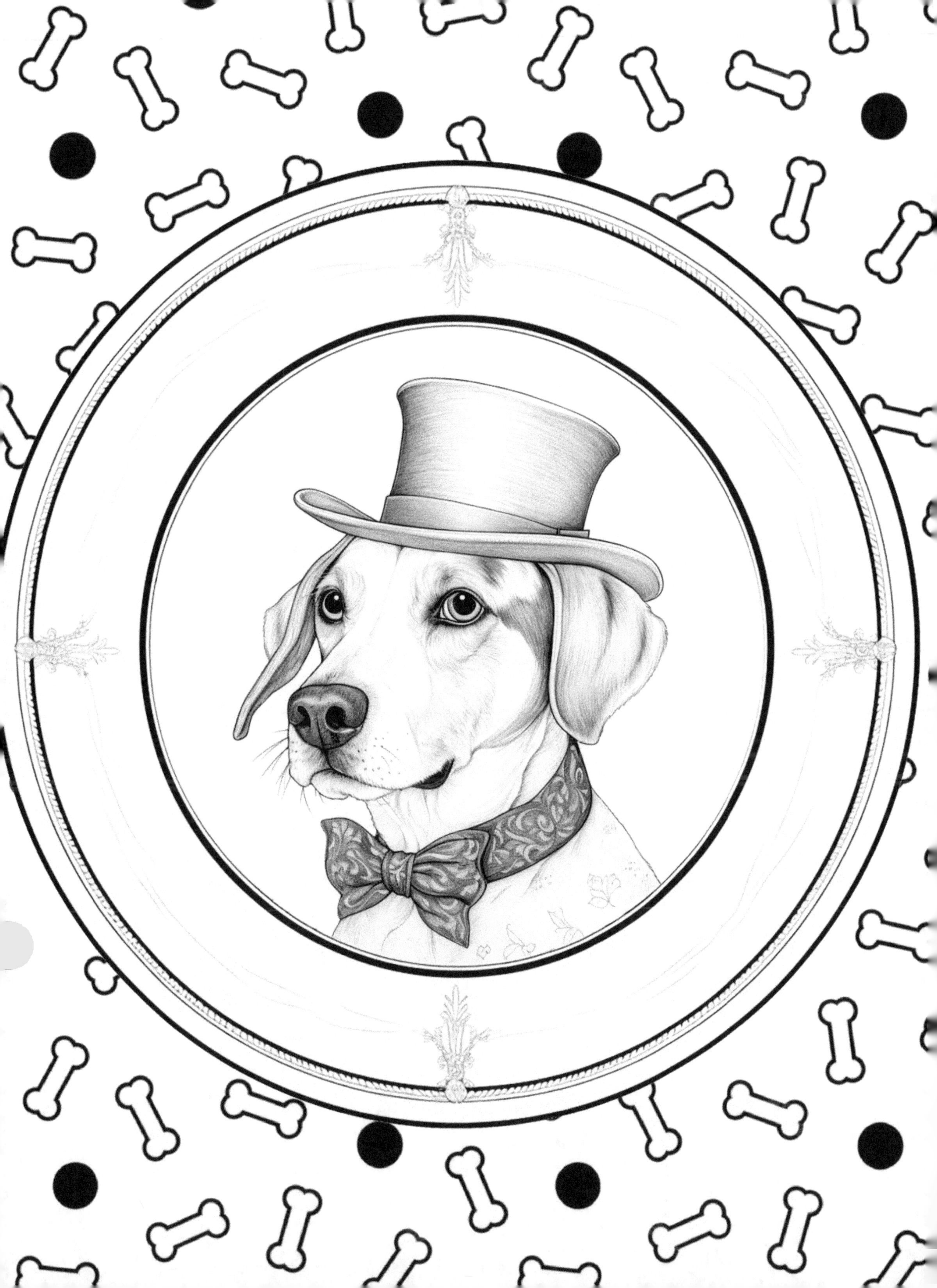

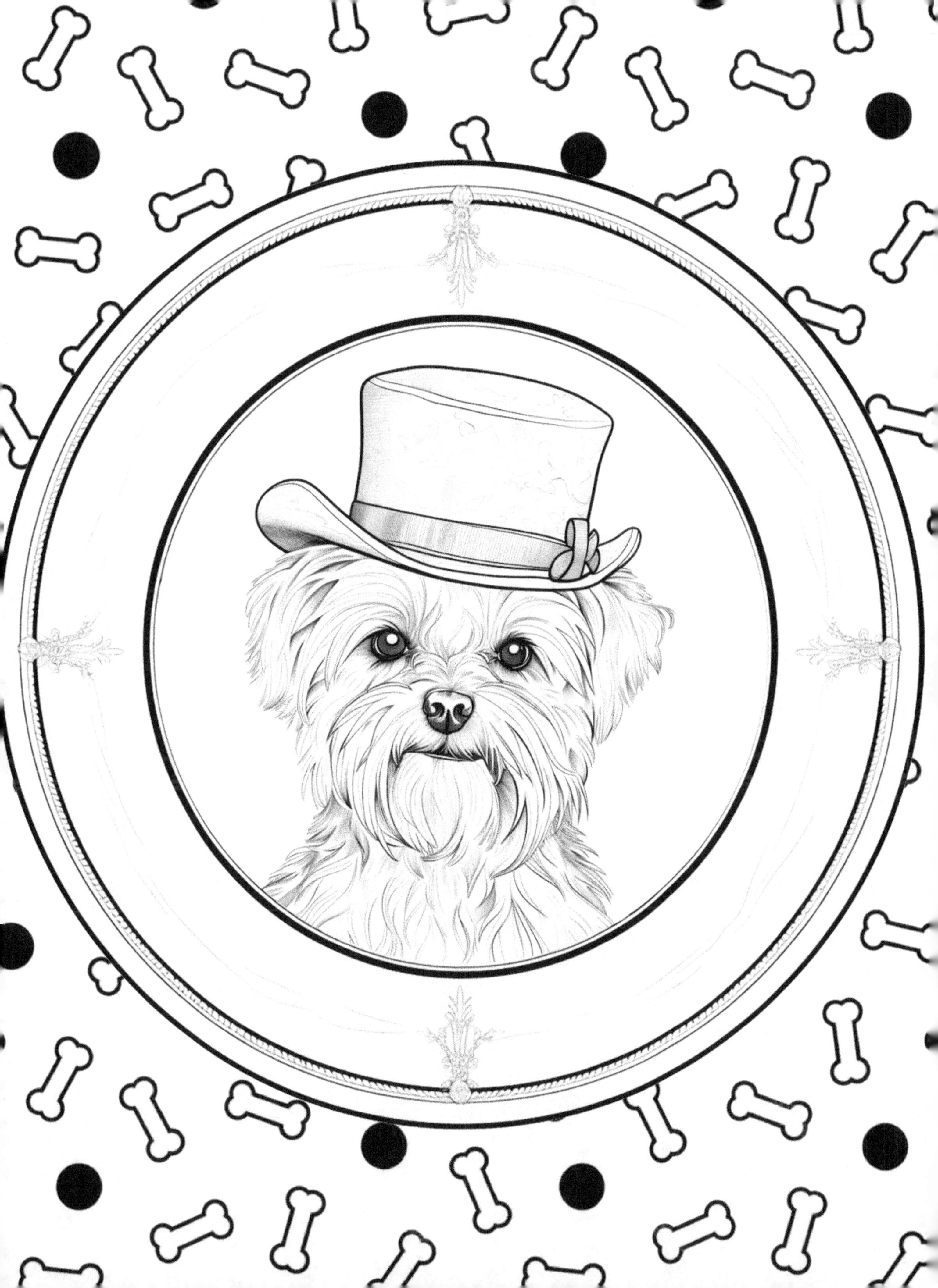

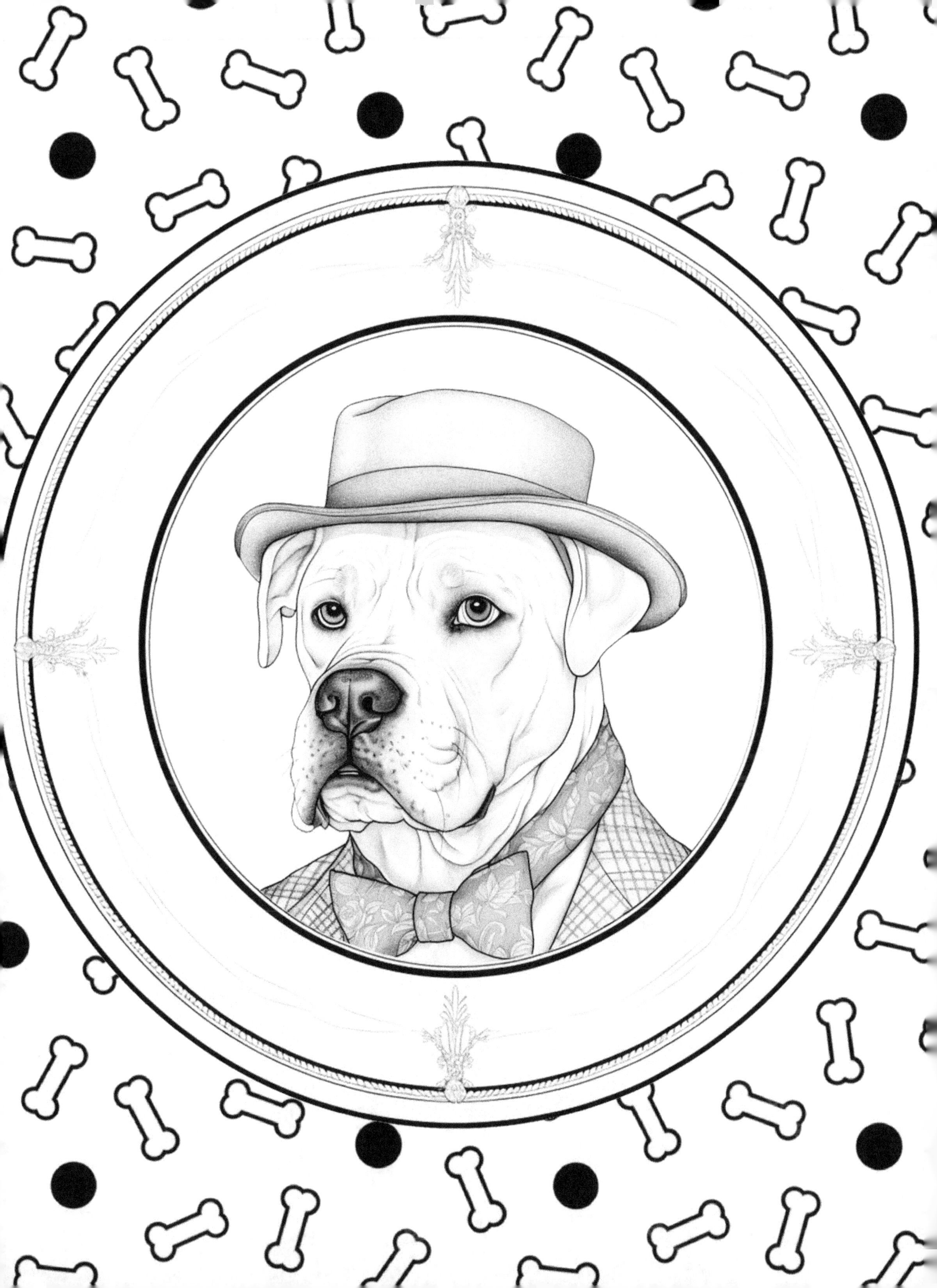

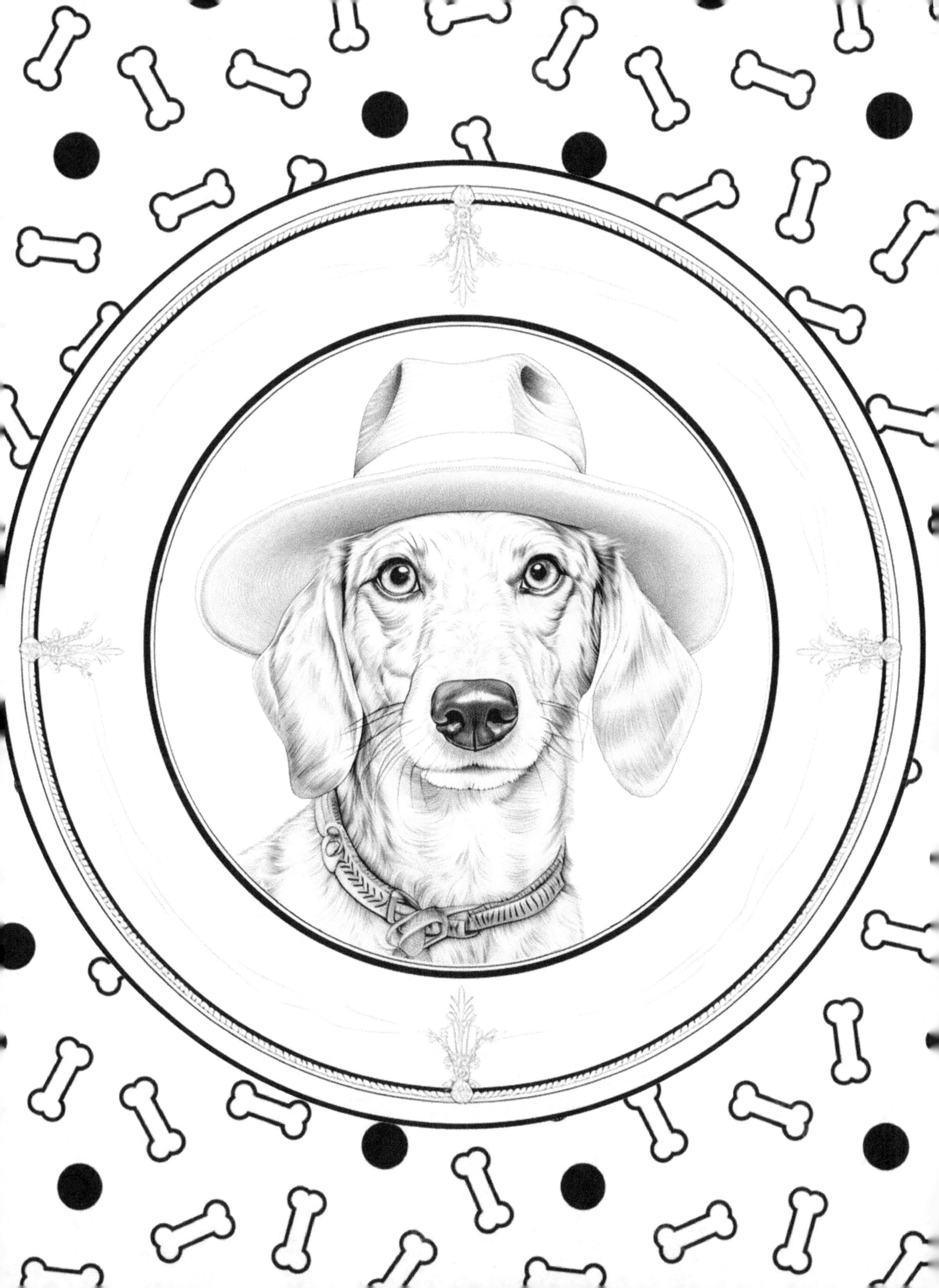

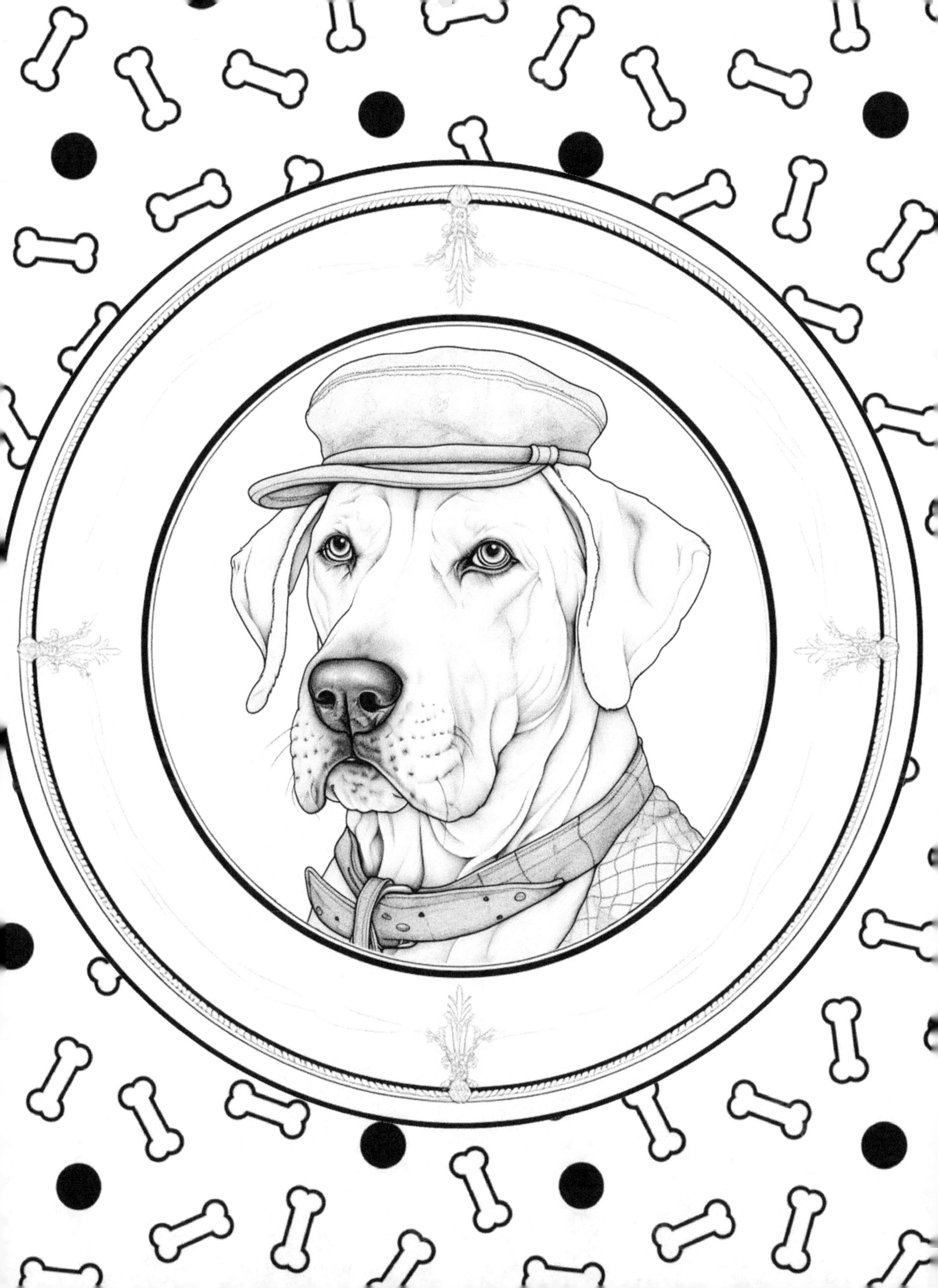

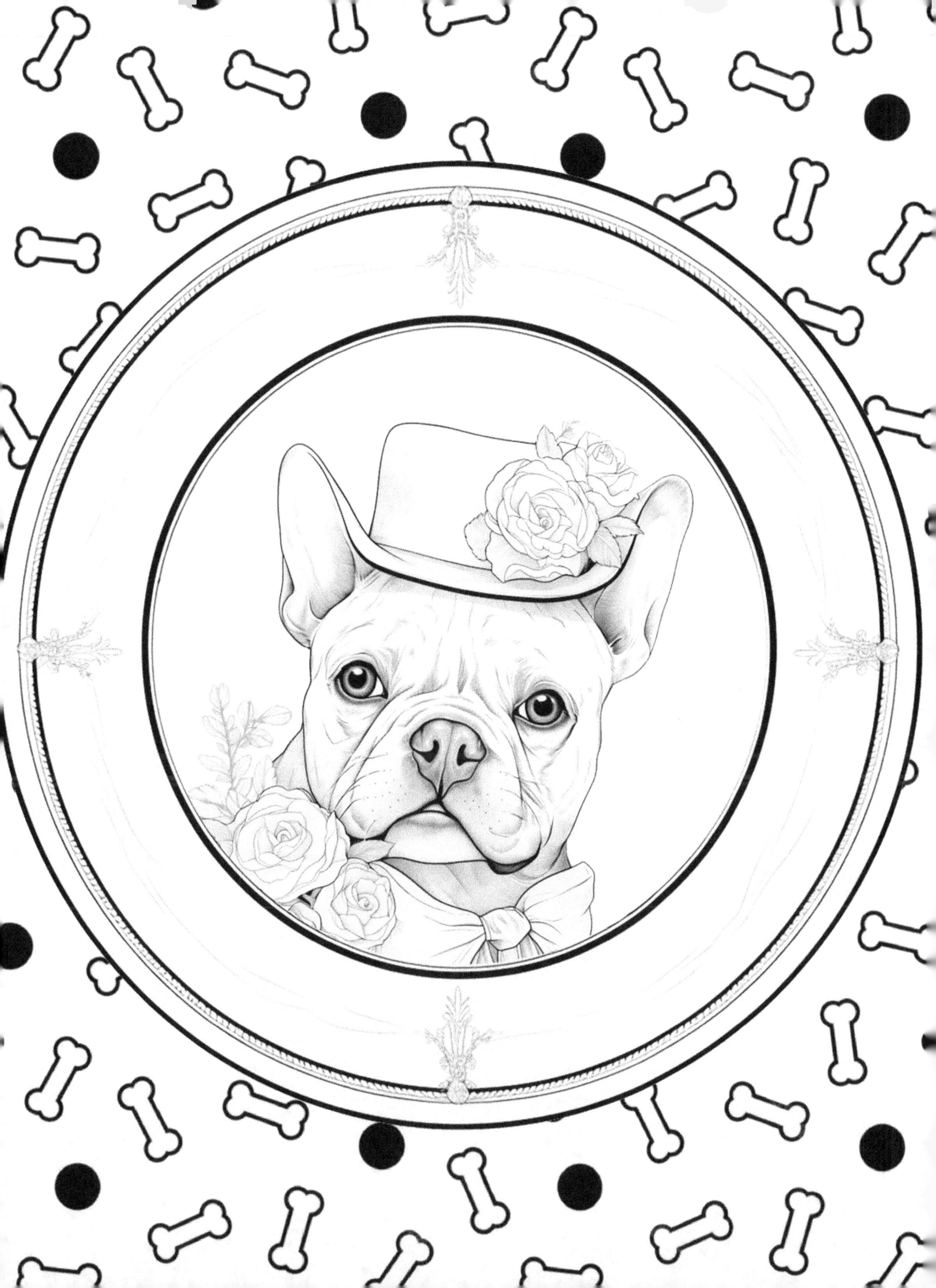

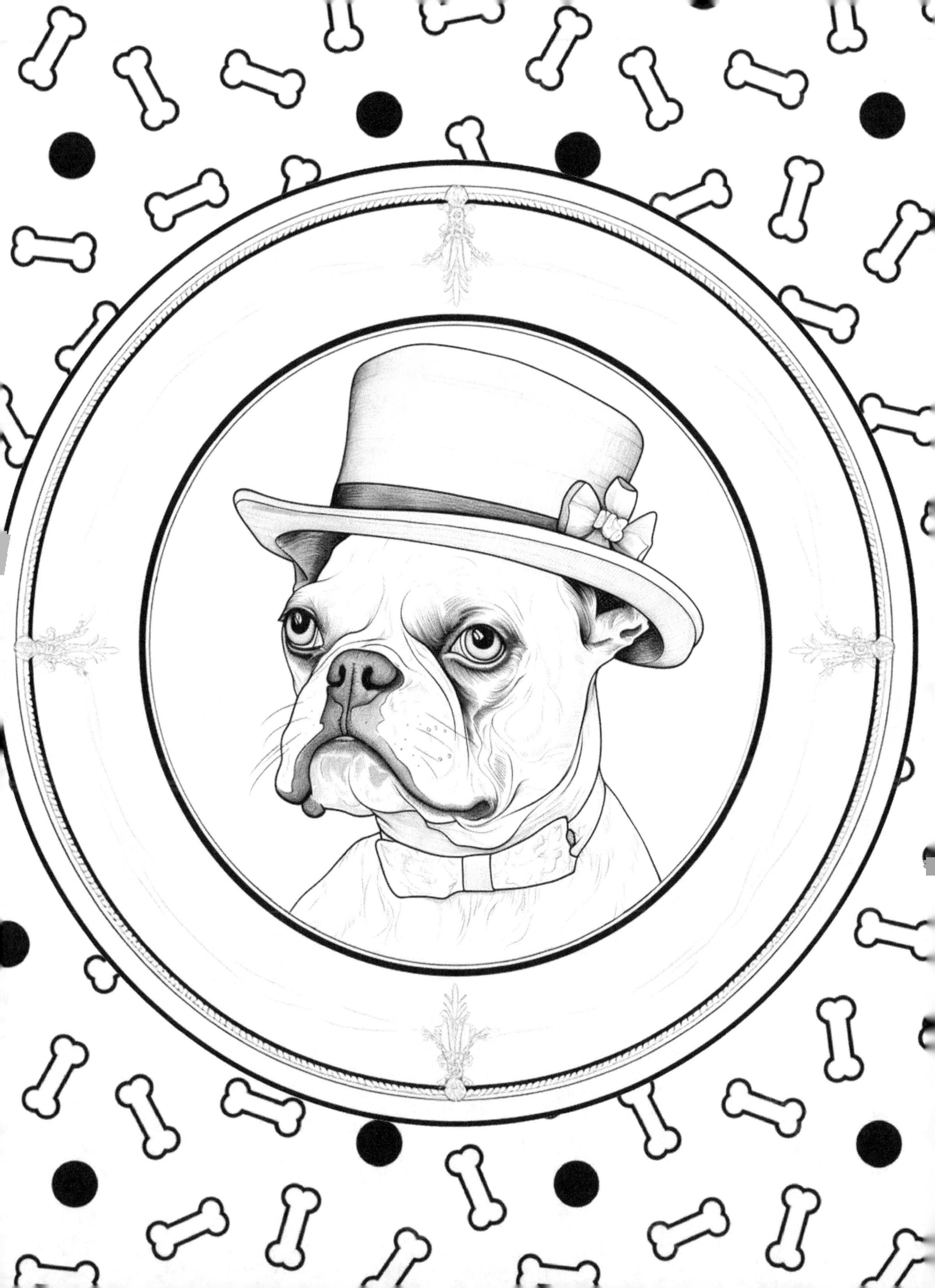

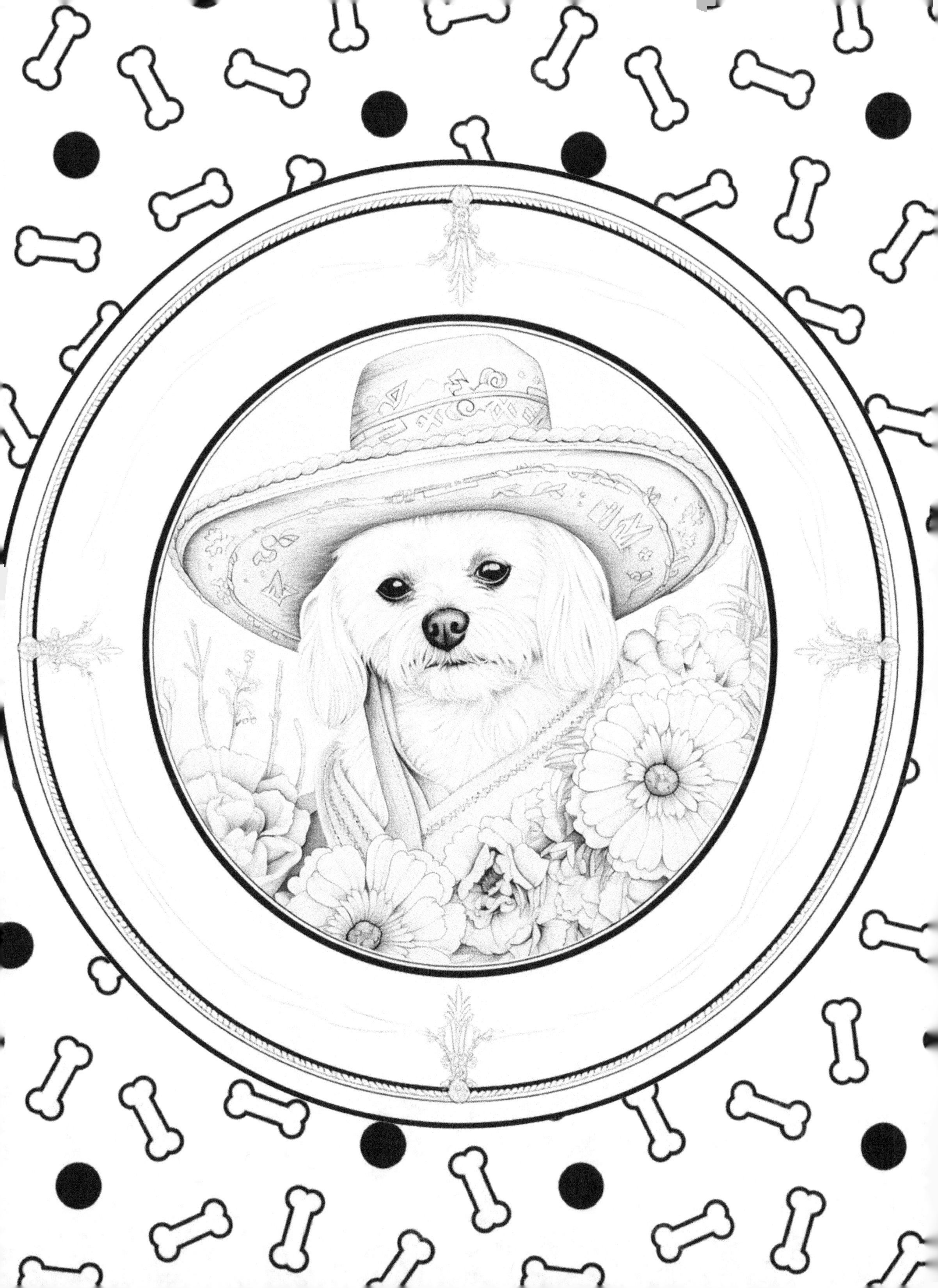

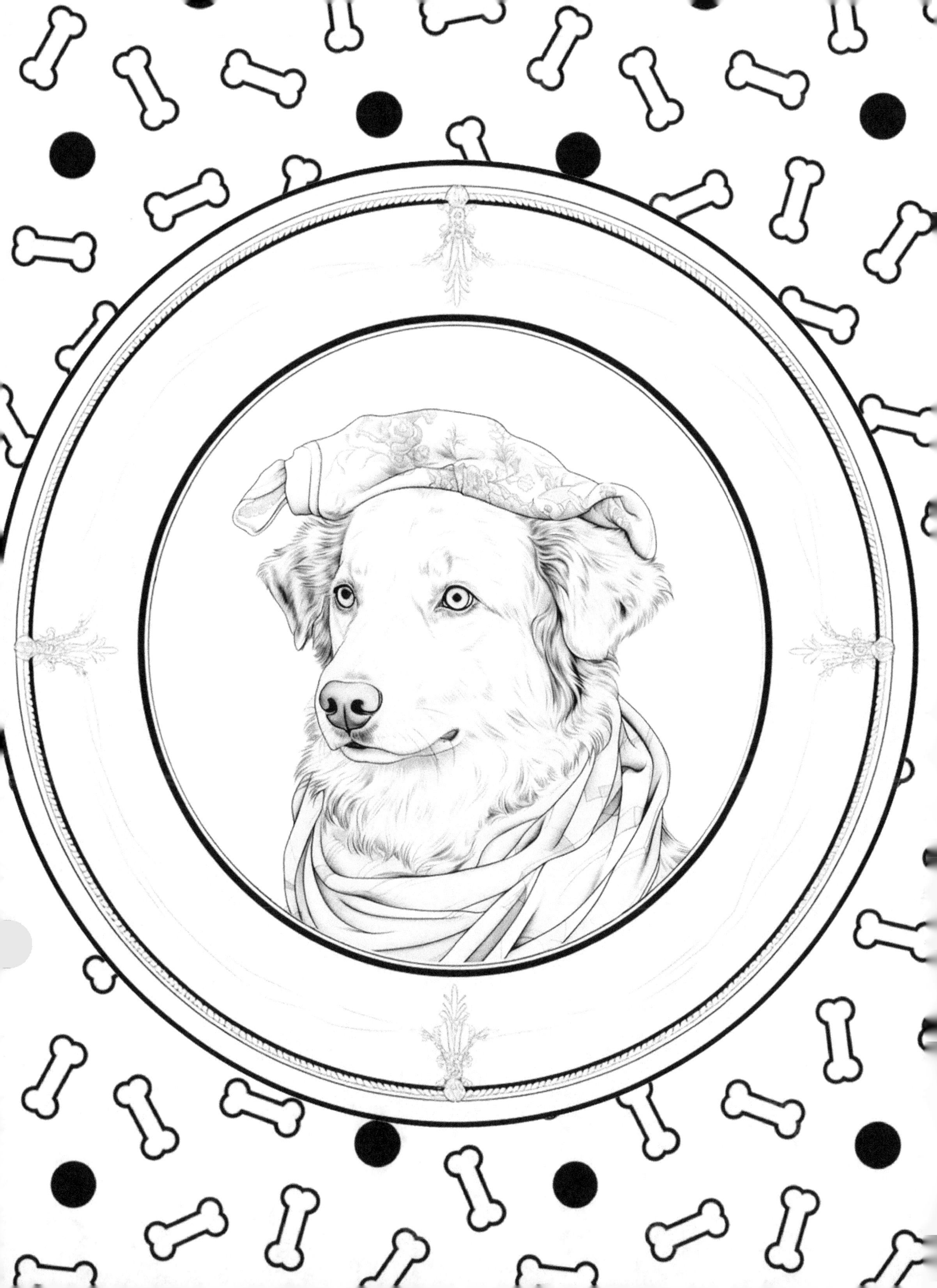

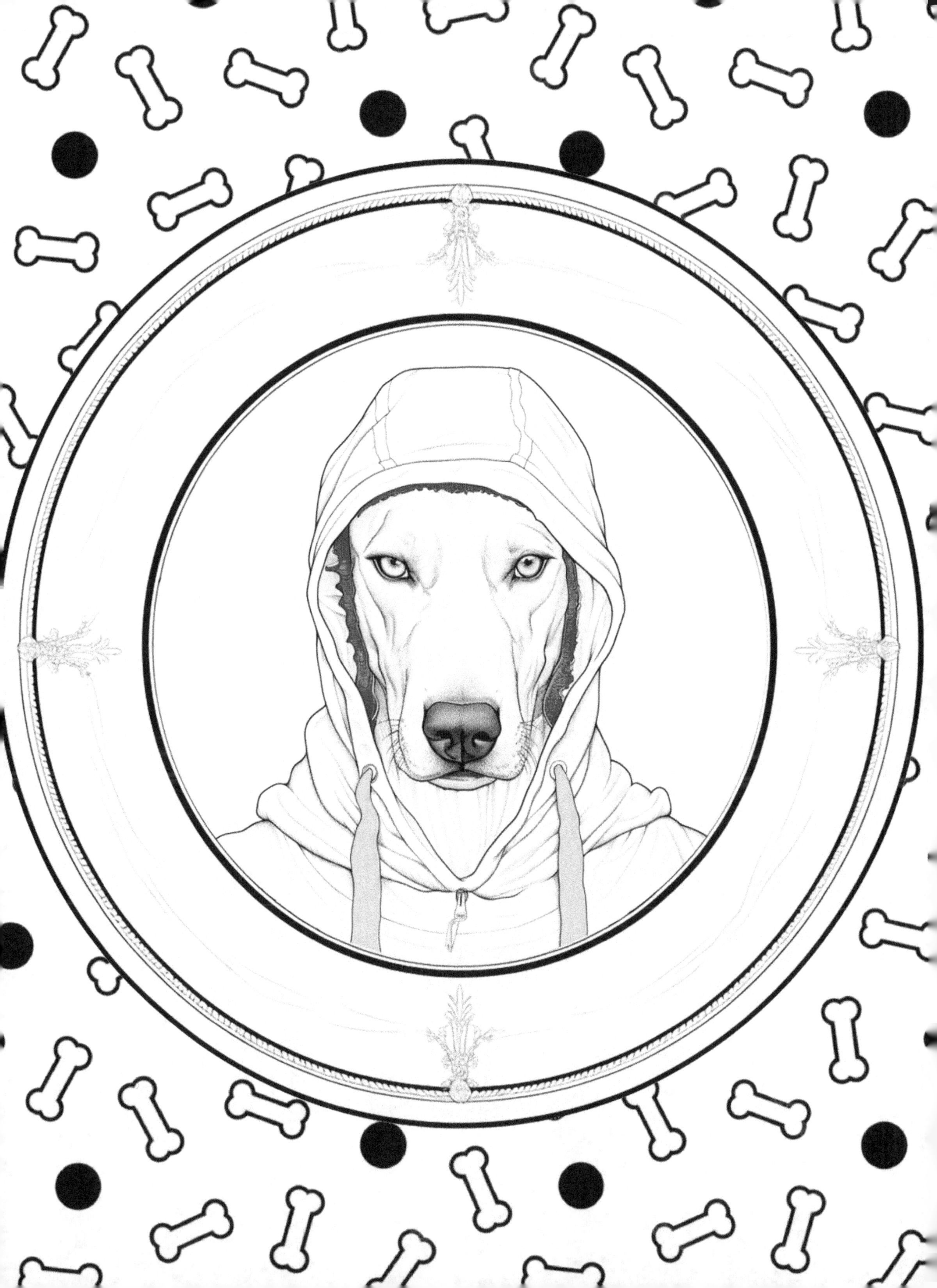

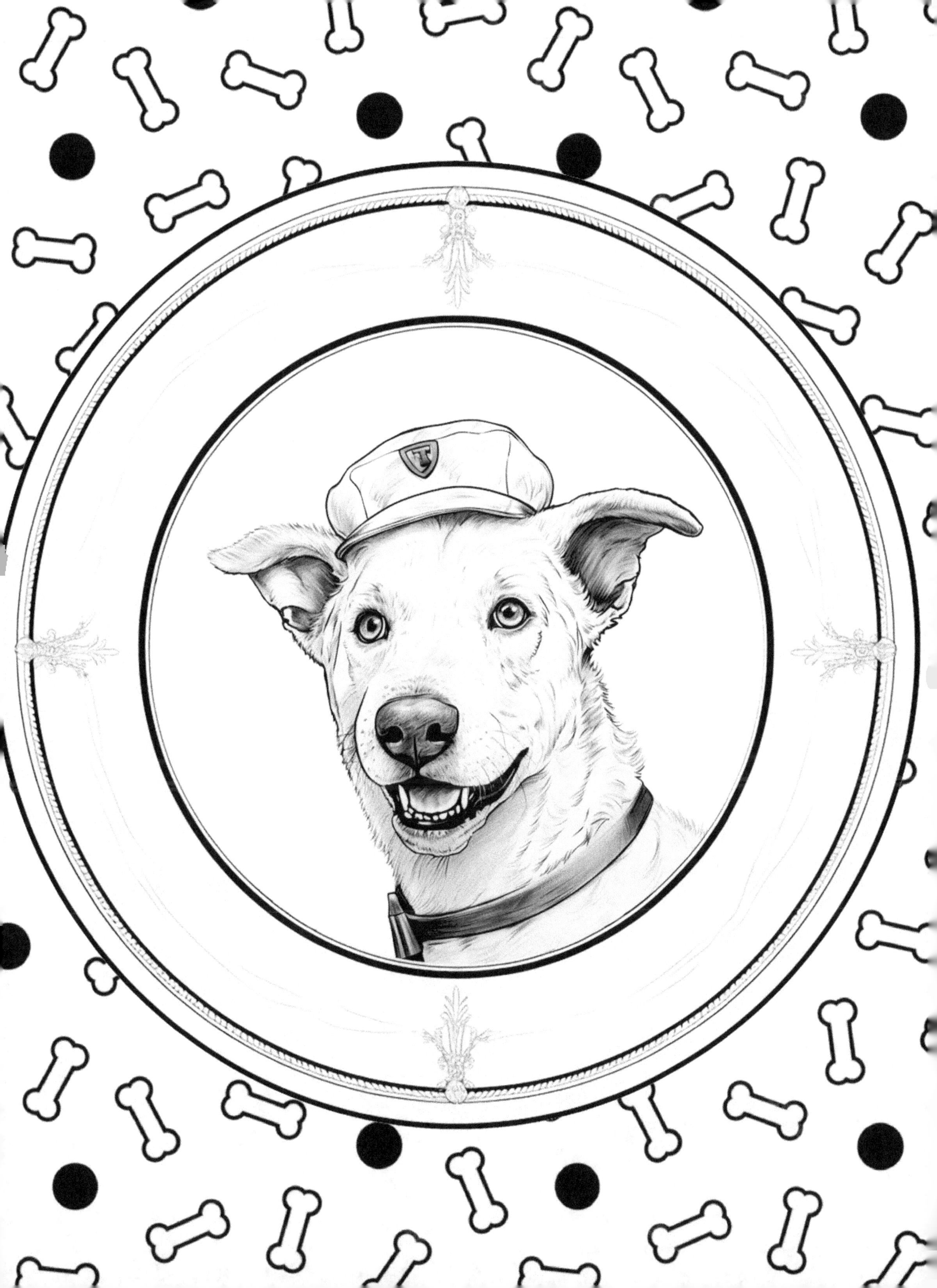

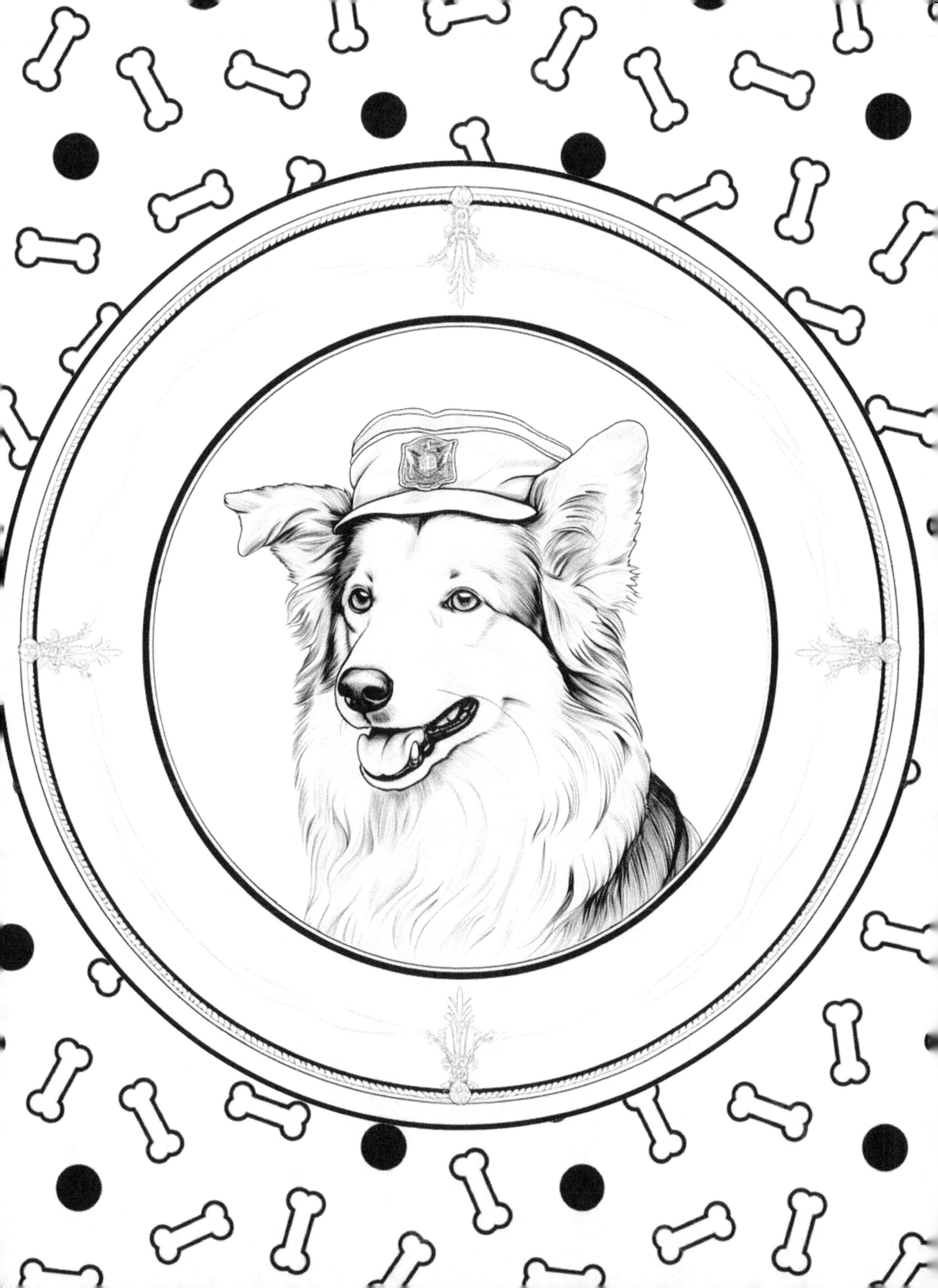

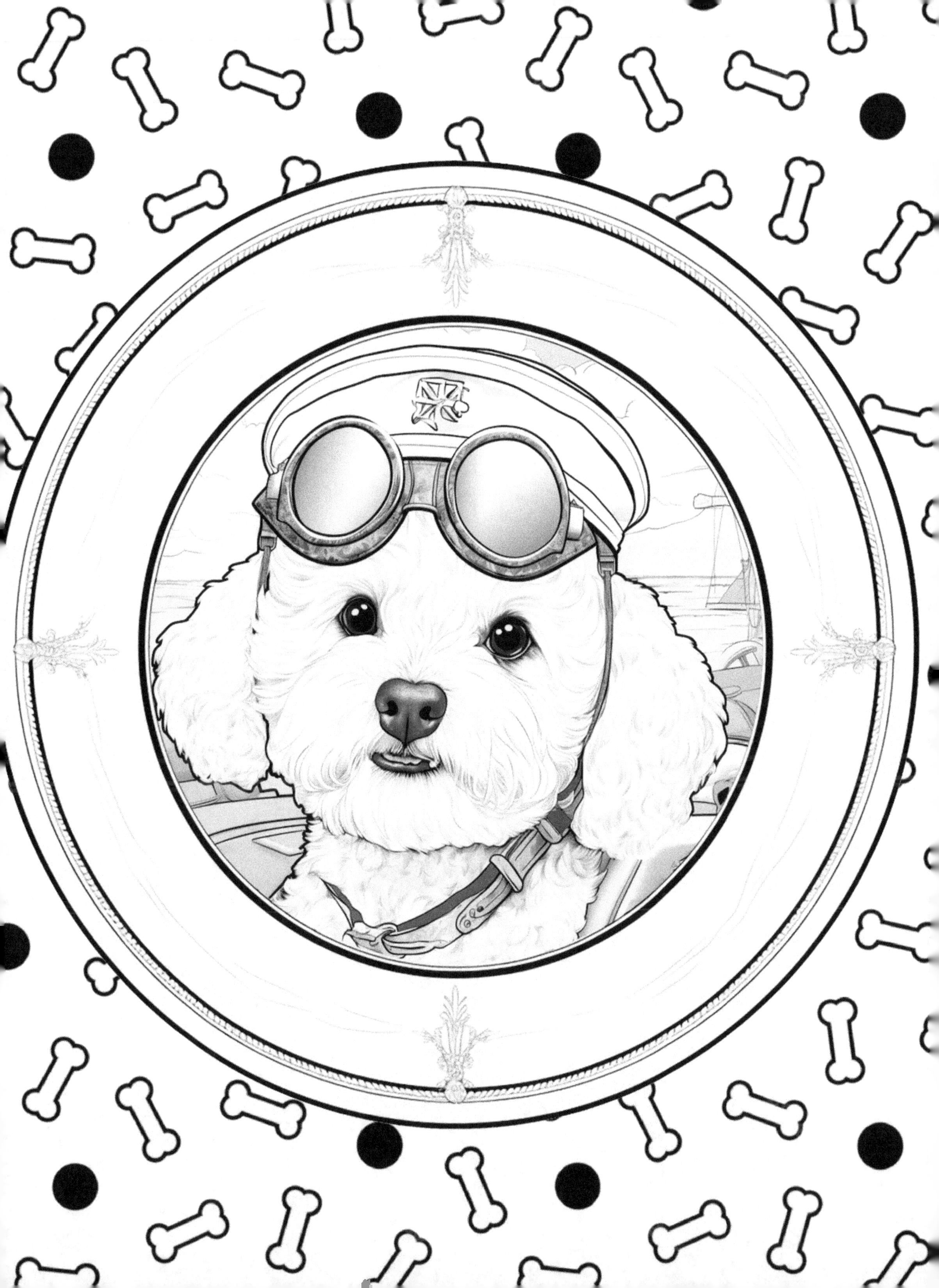

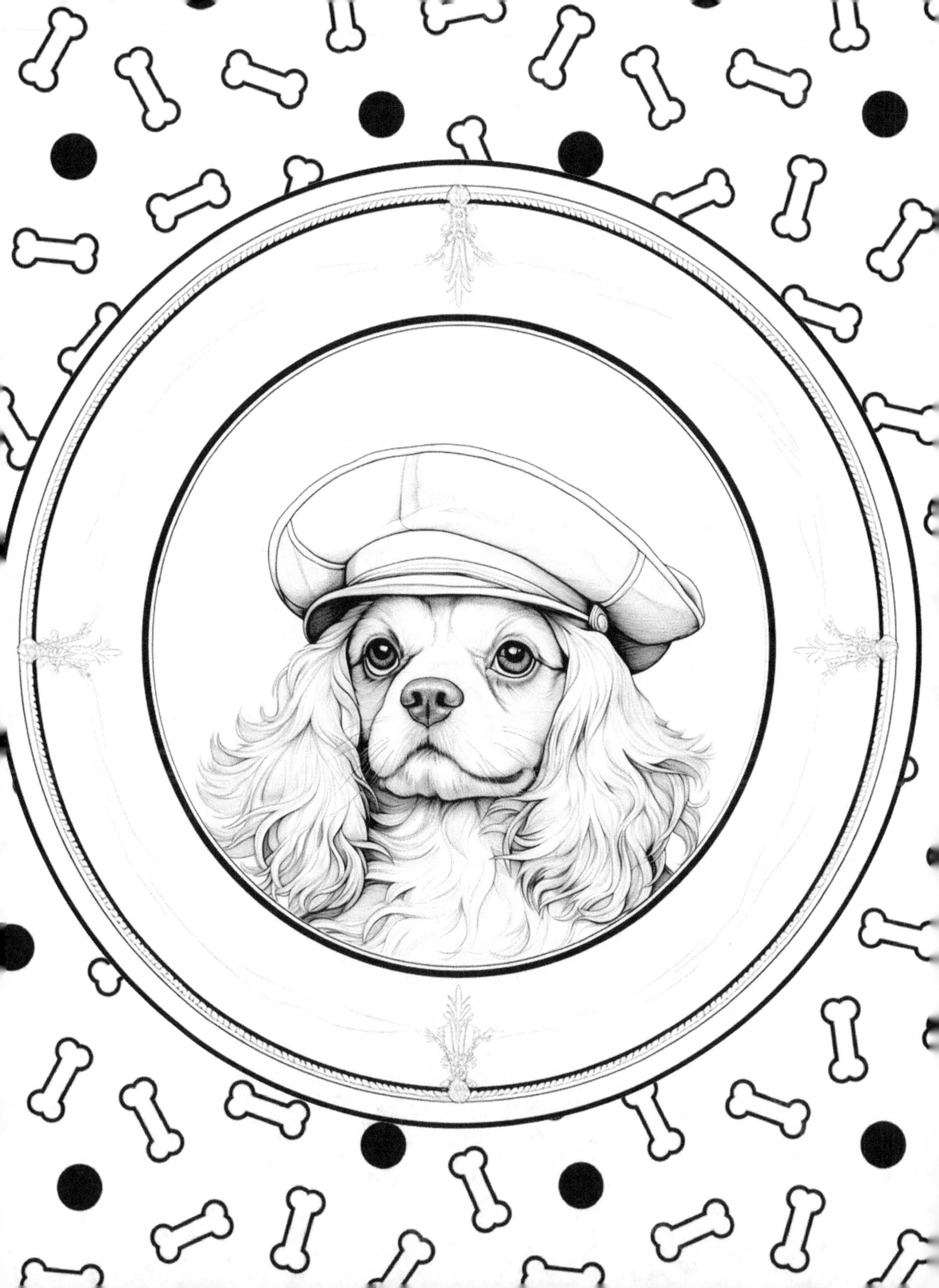

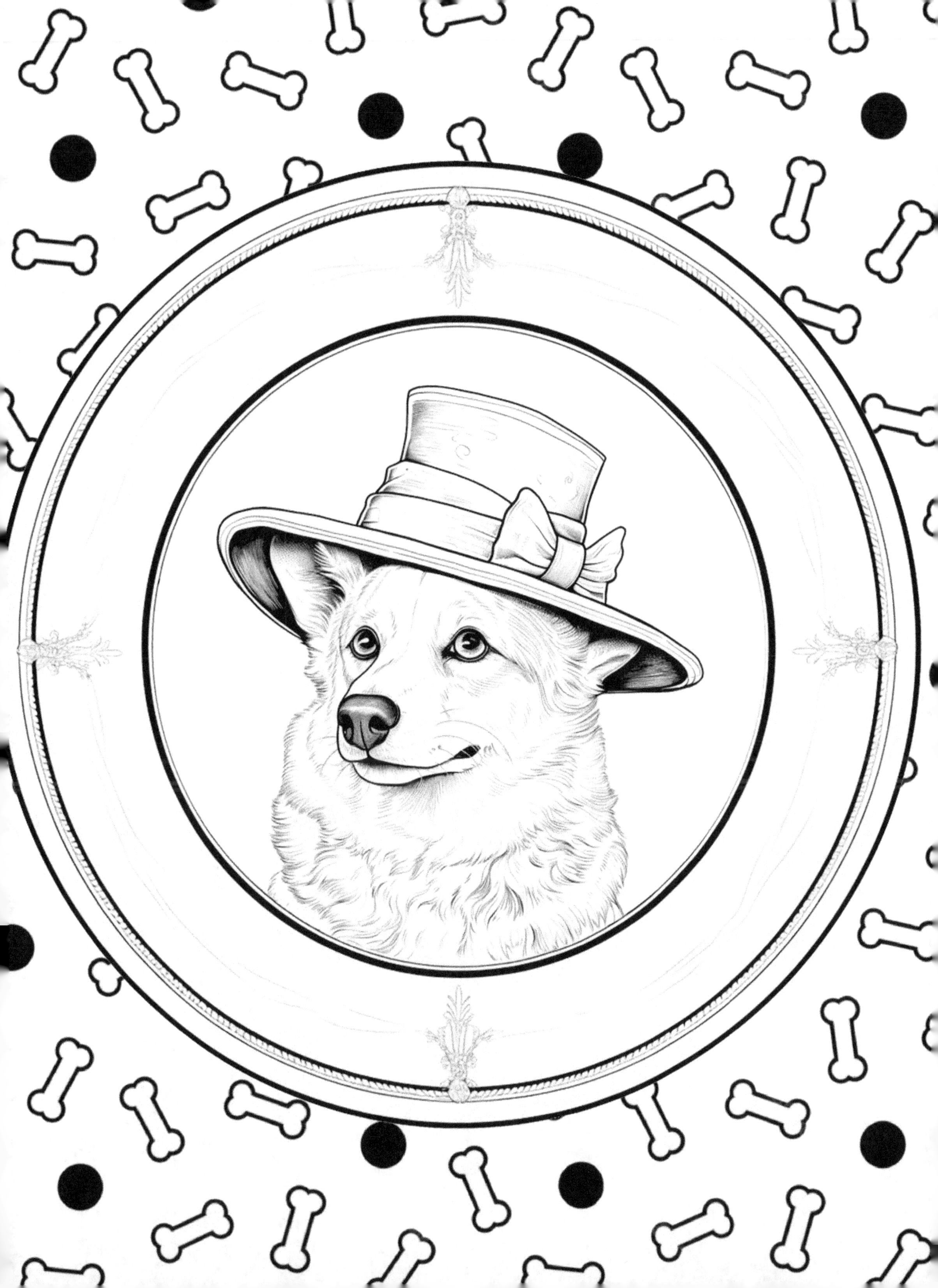

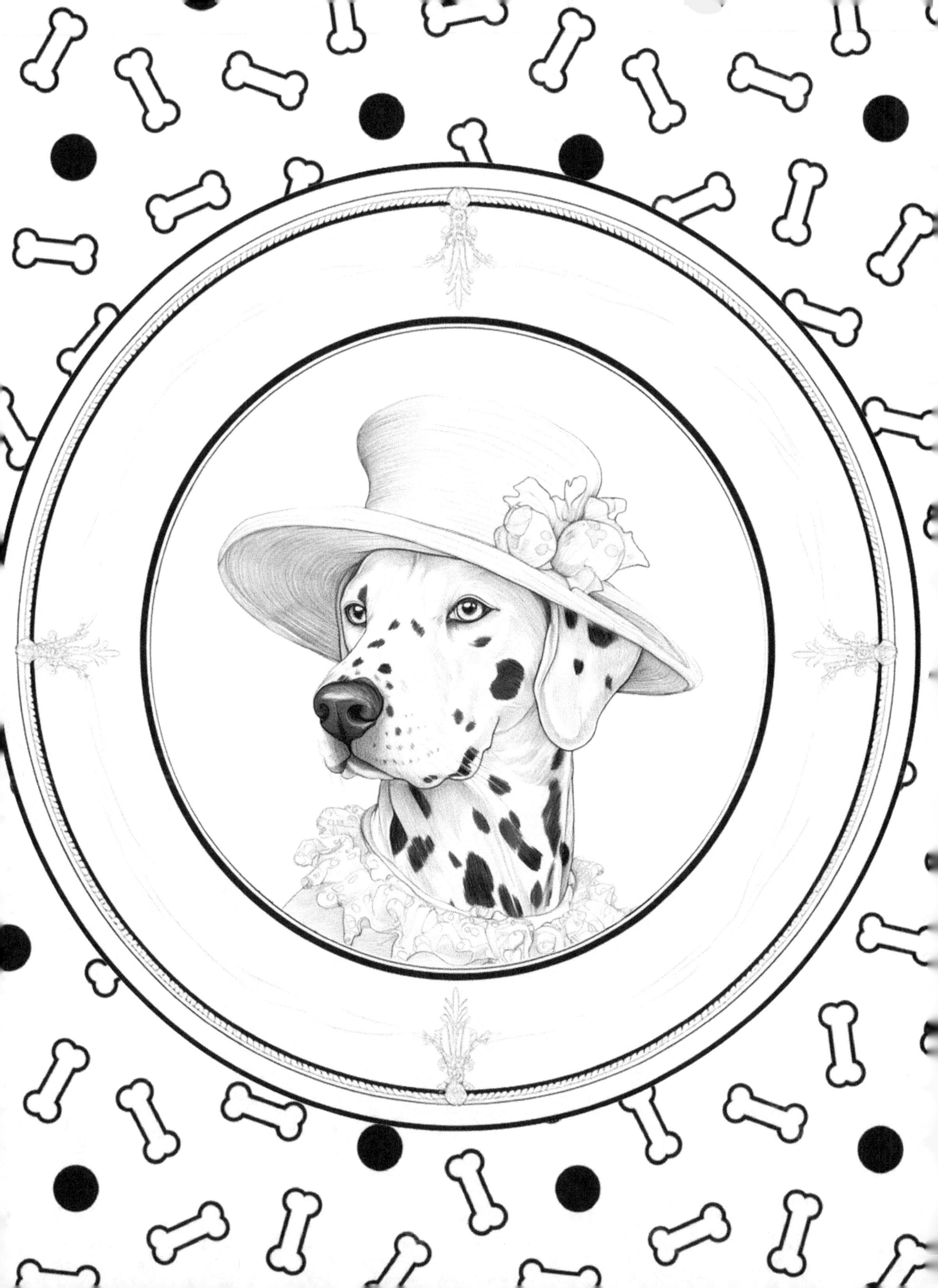

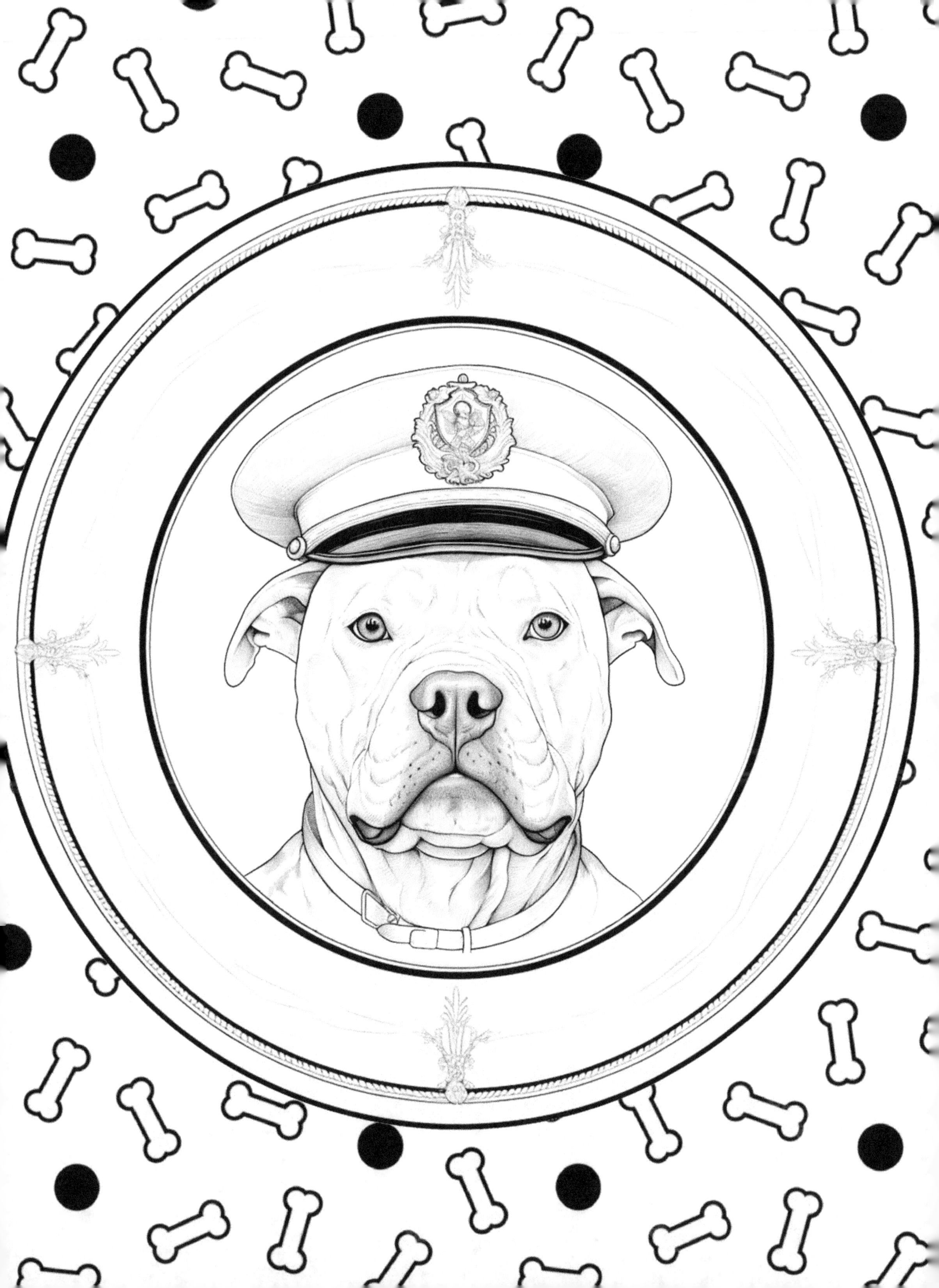

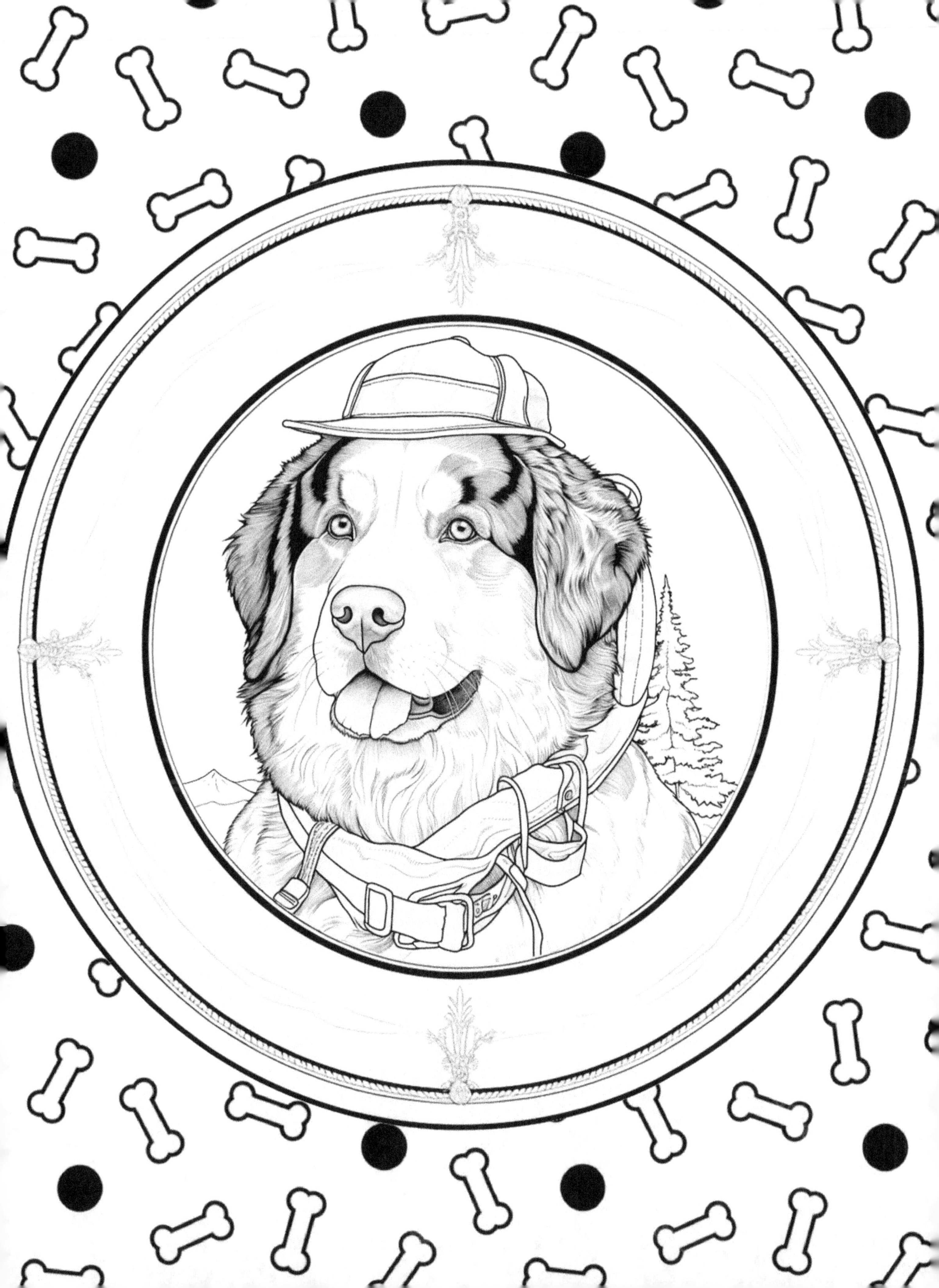

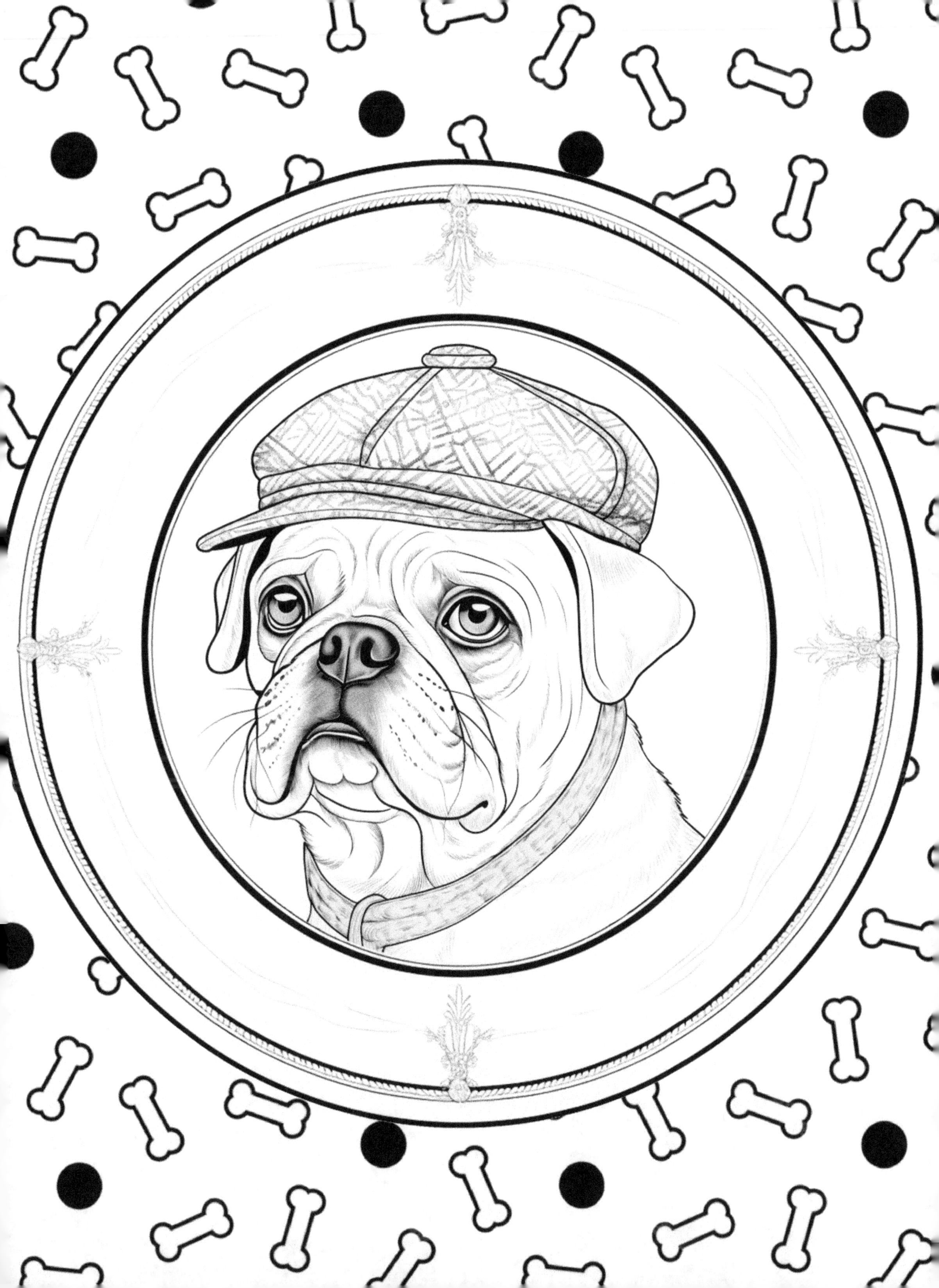

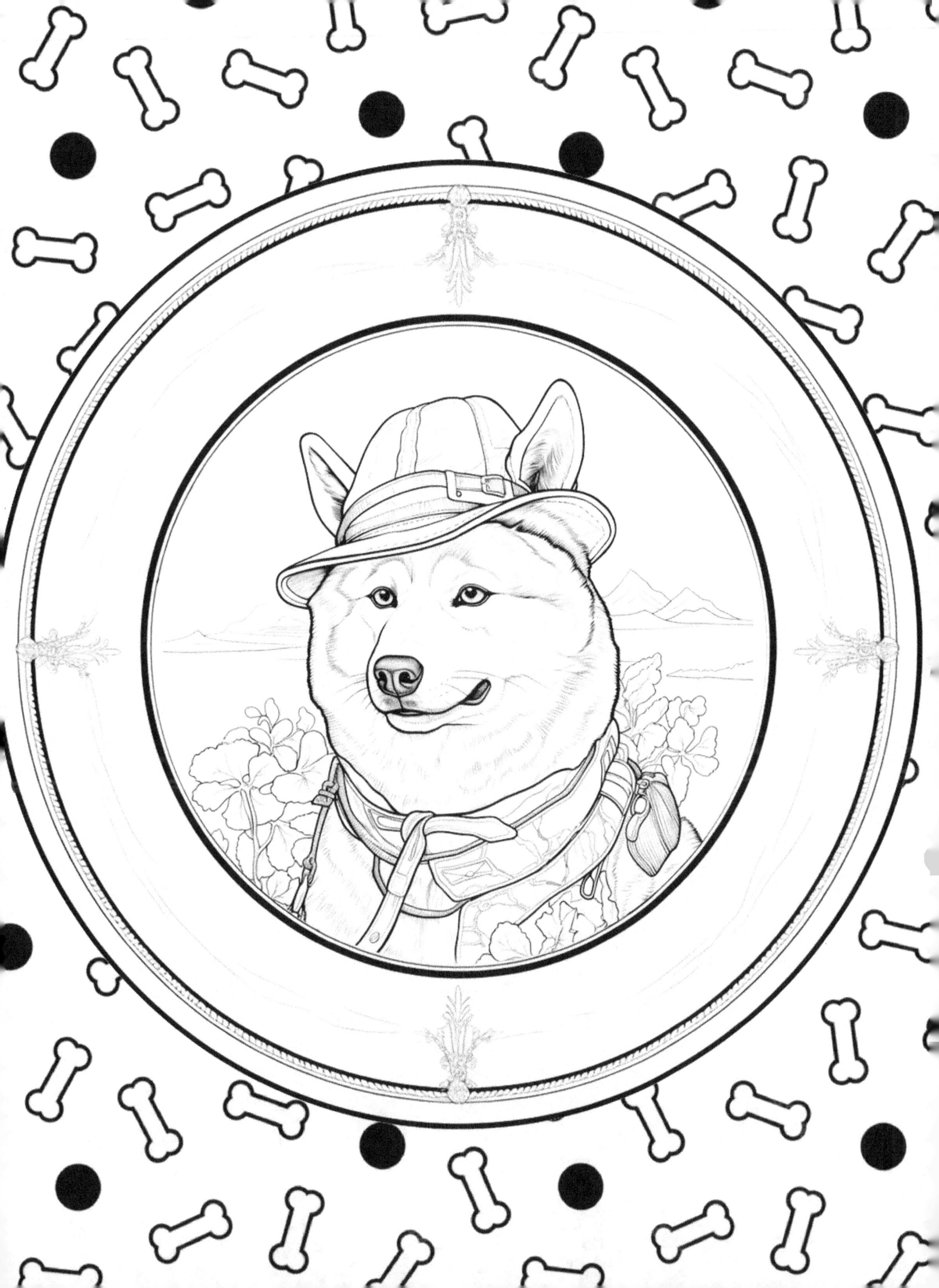

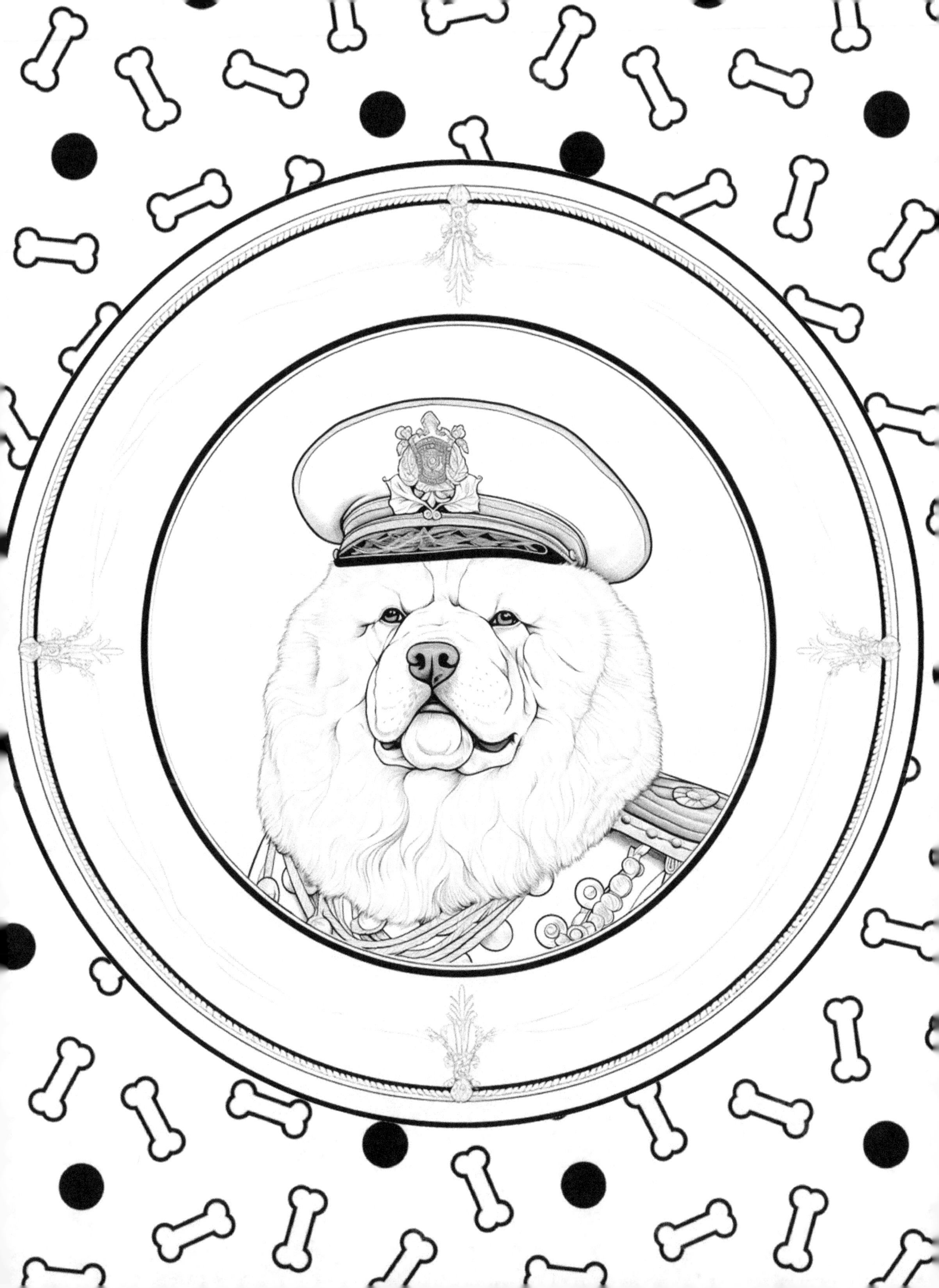

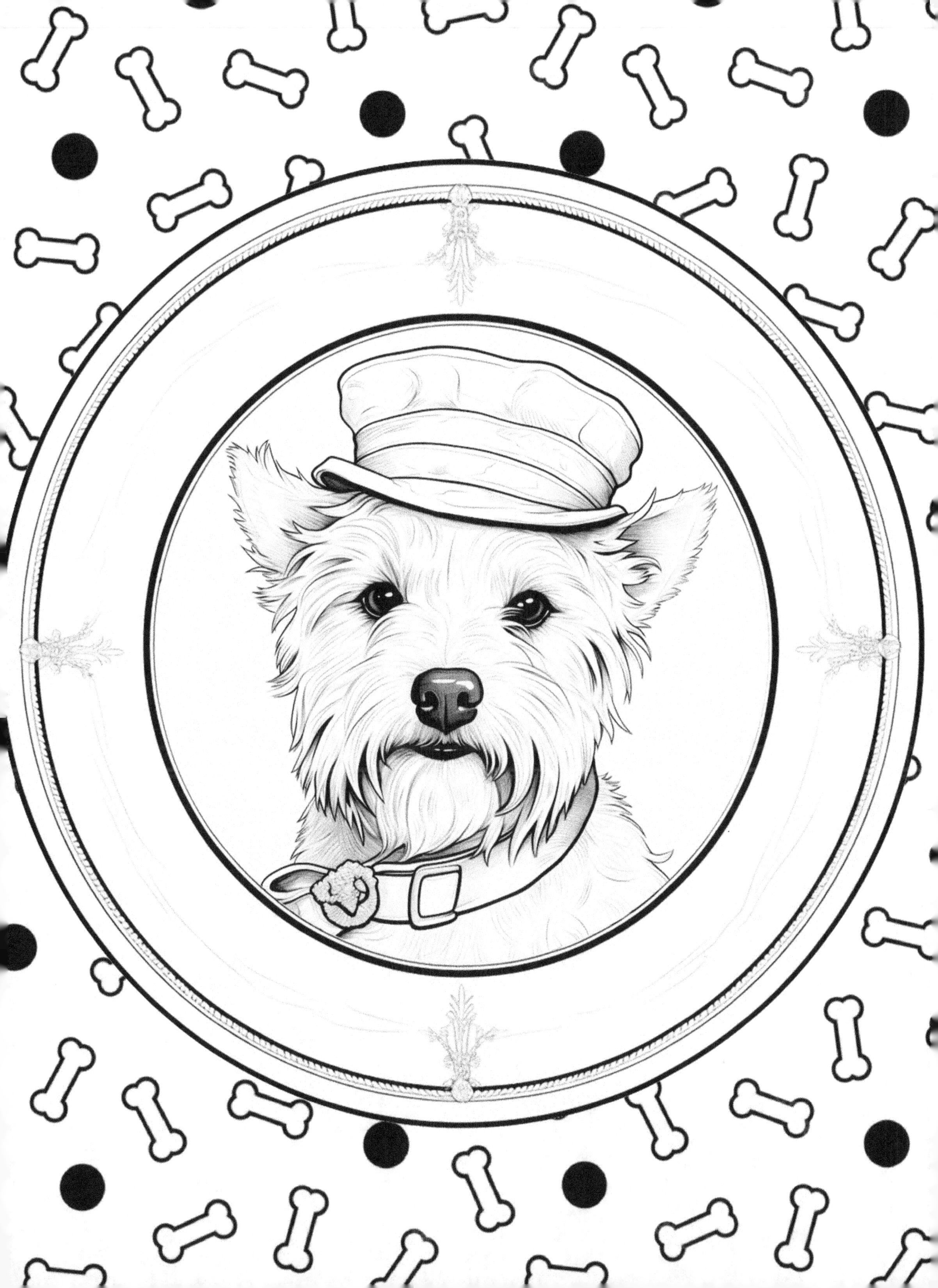

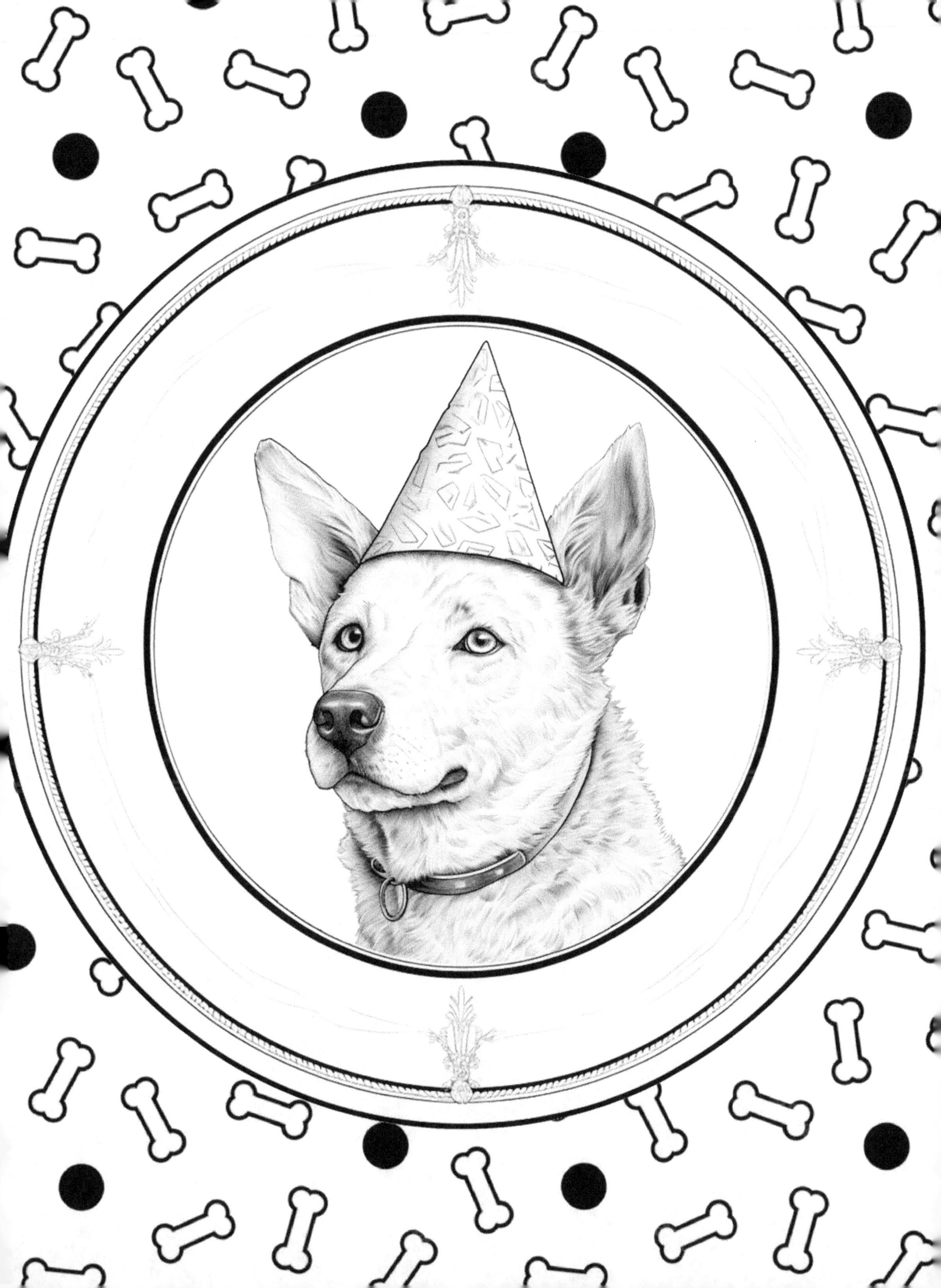

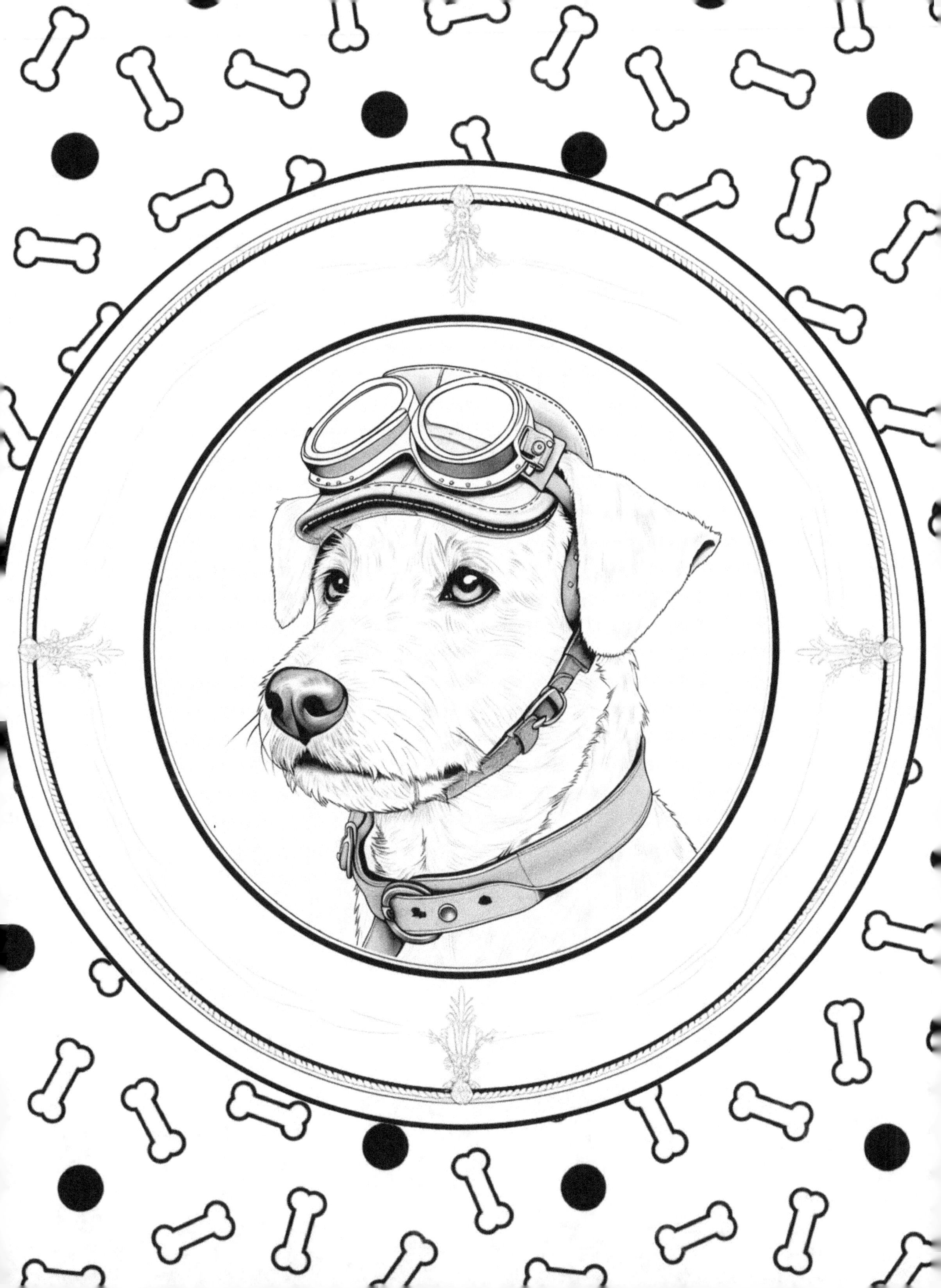

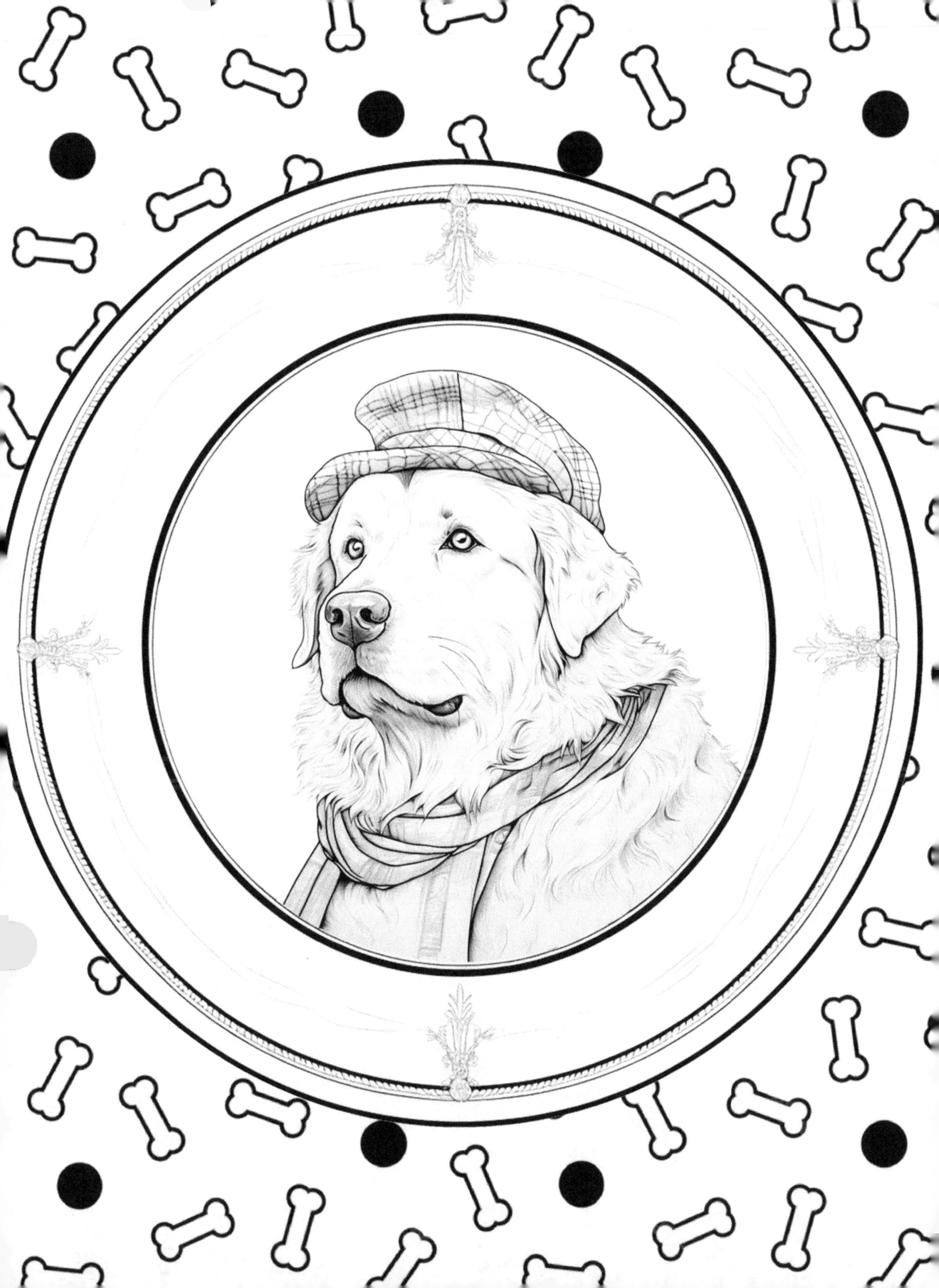

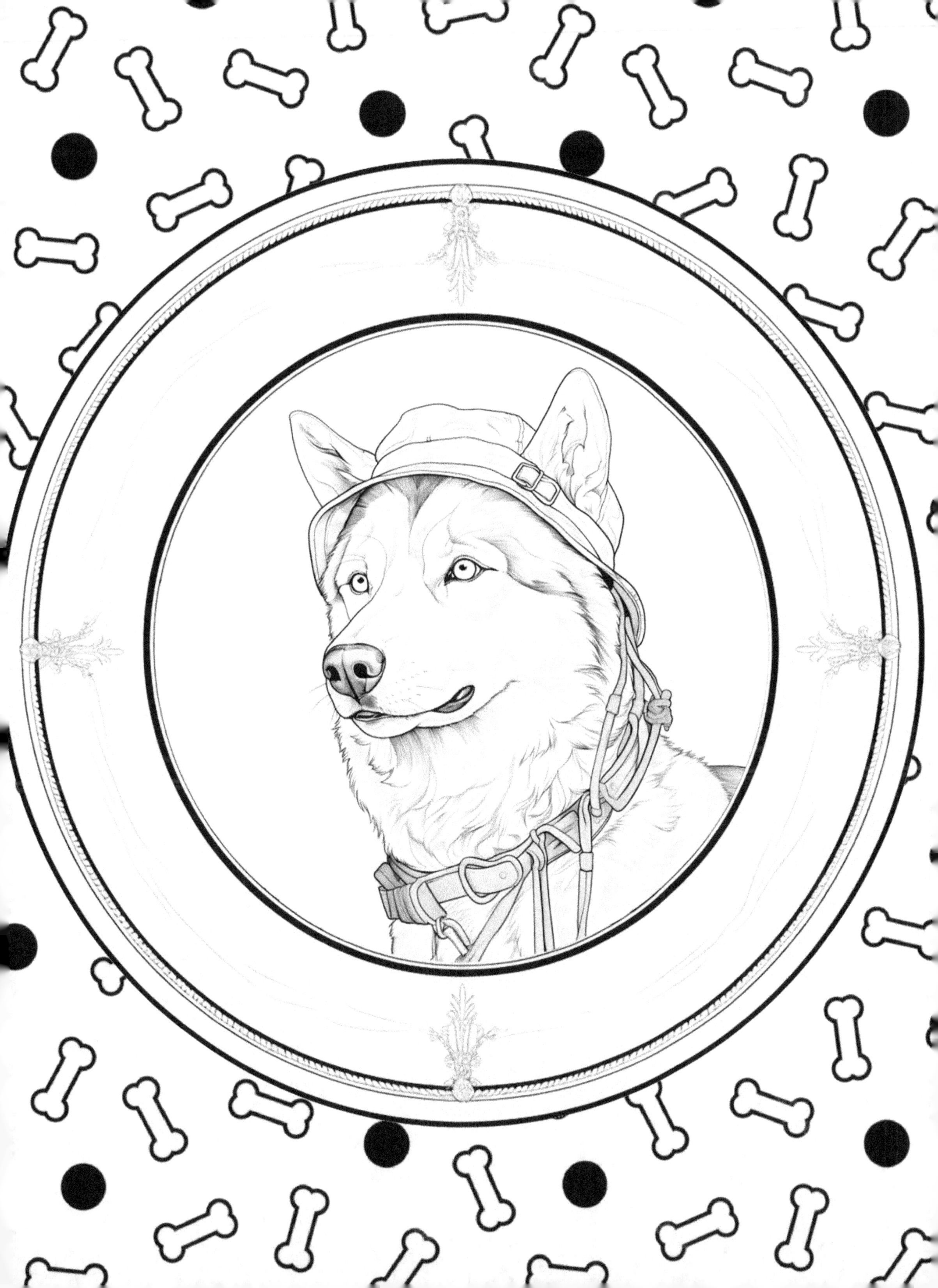

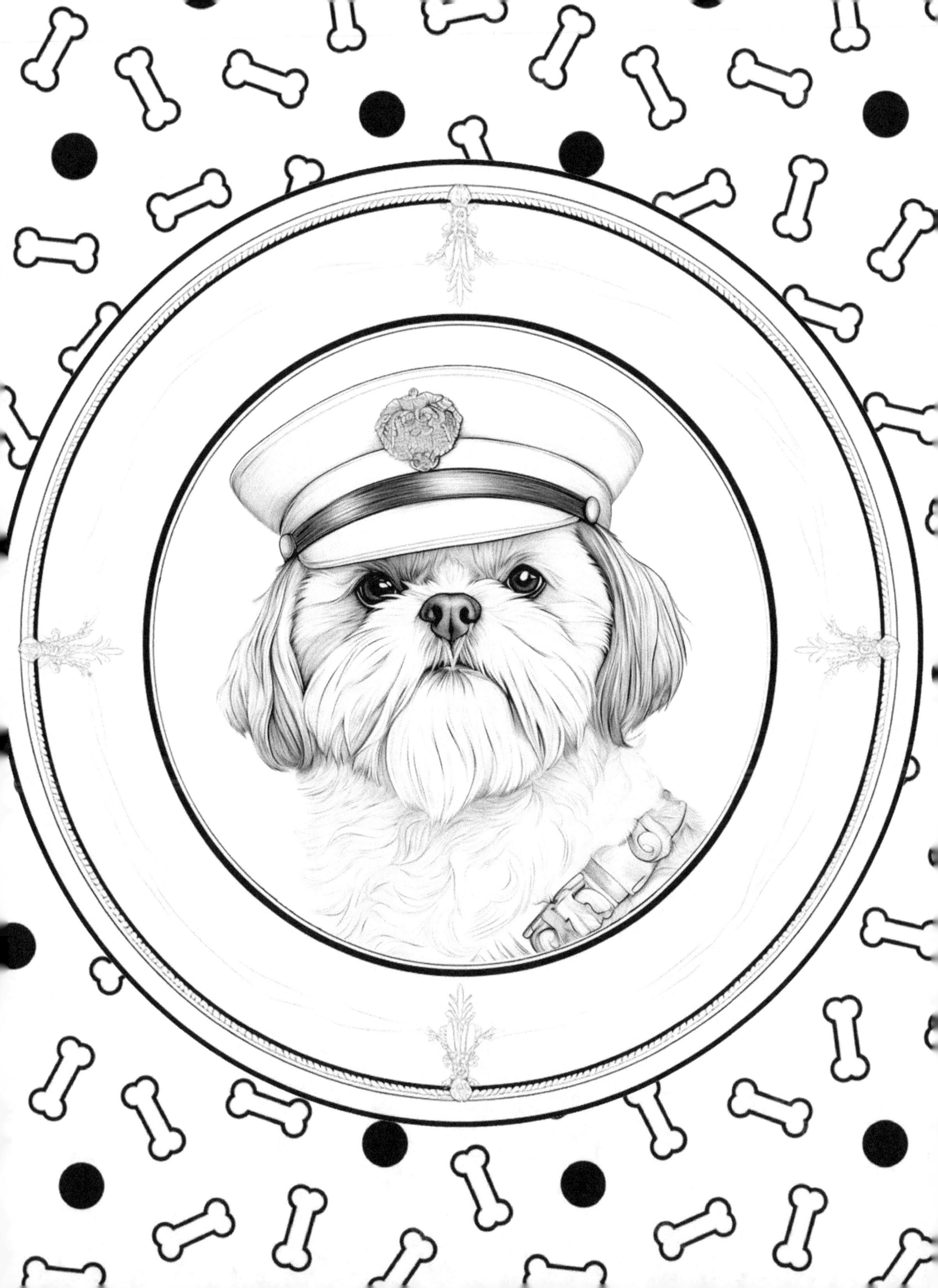

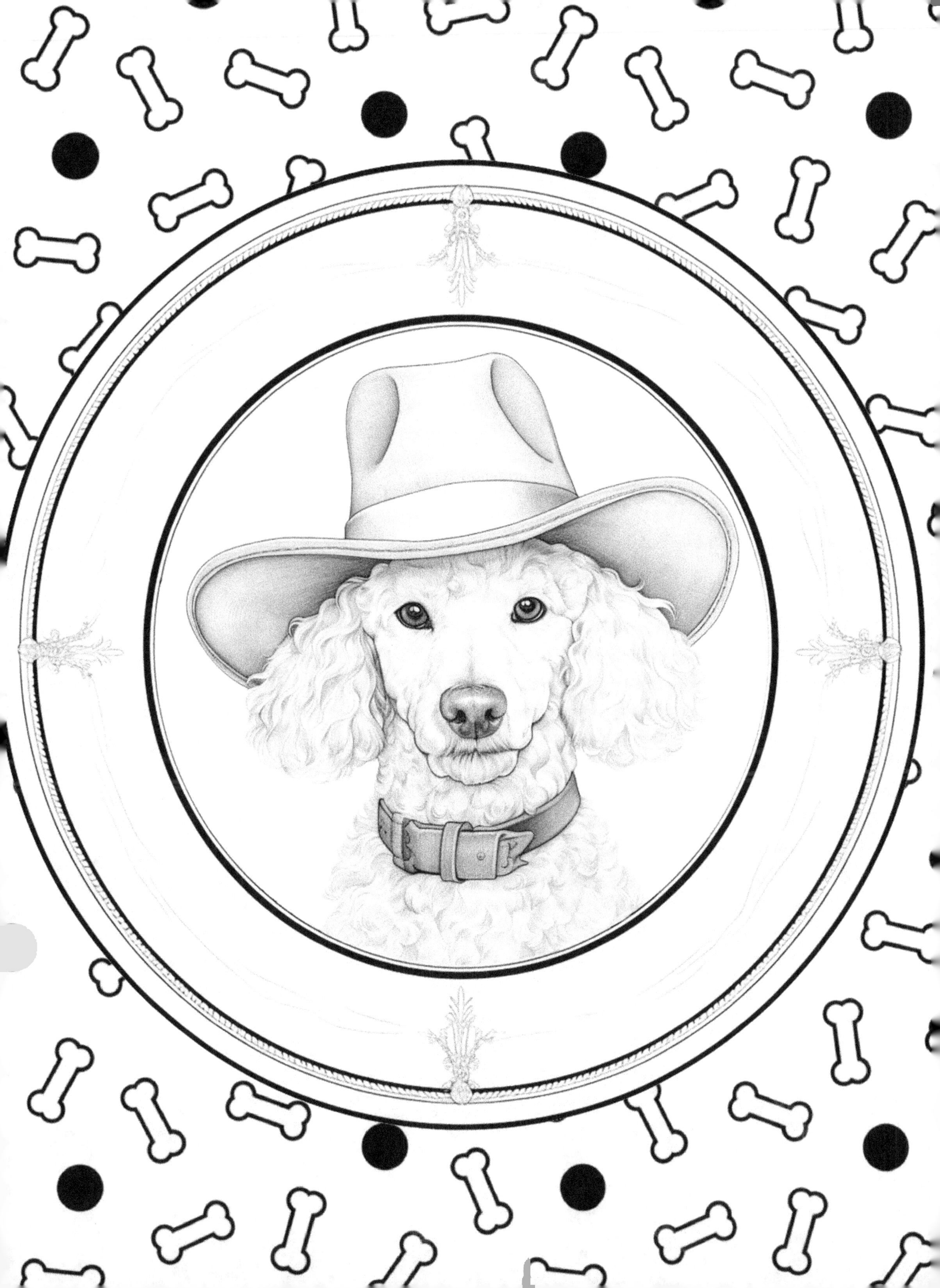

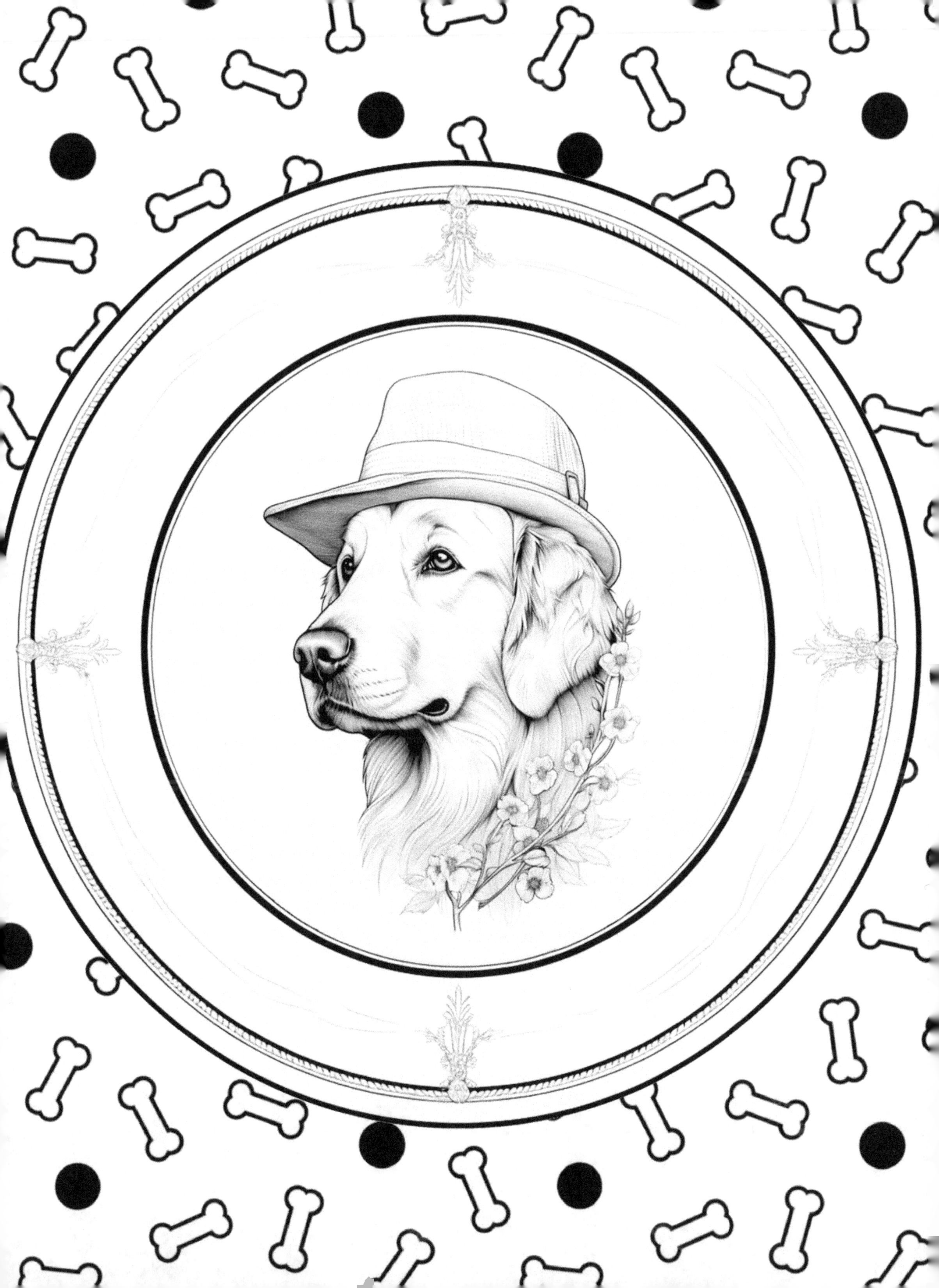

COLOR TEST PAGE

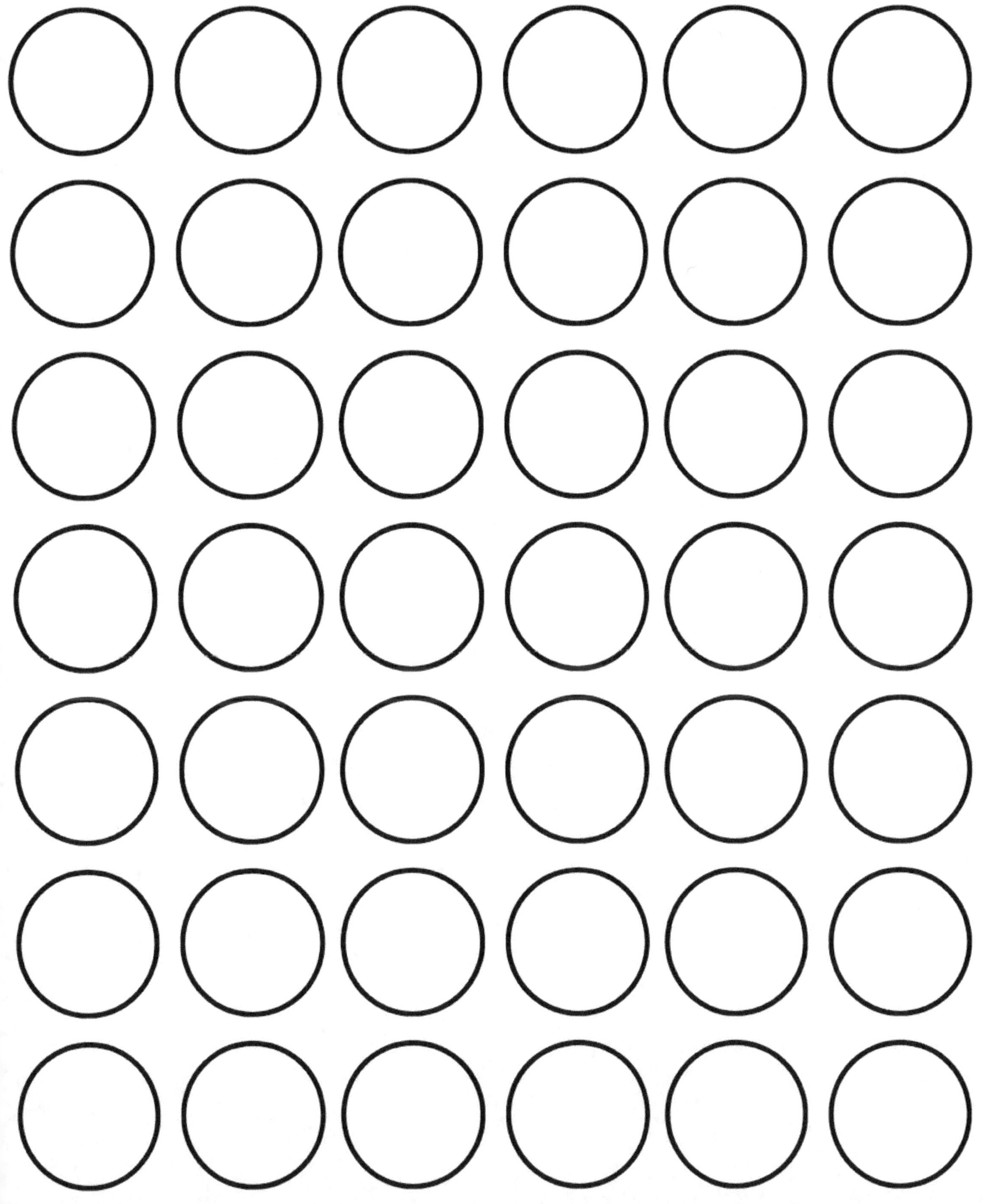

COLOR TEST PAGE

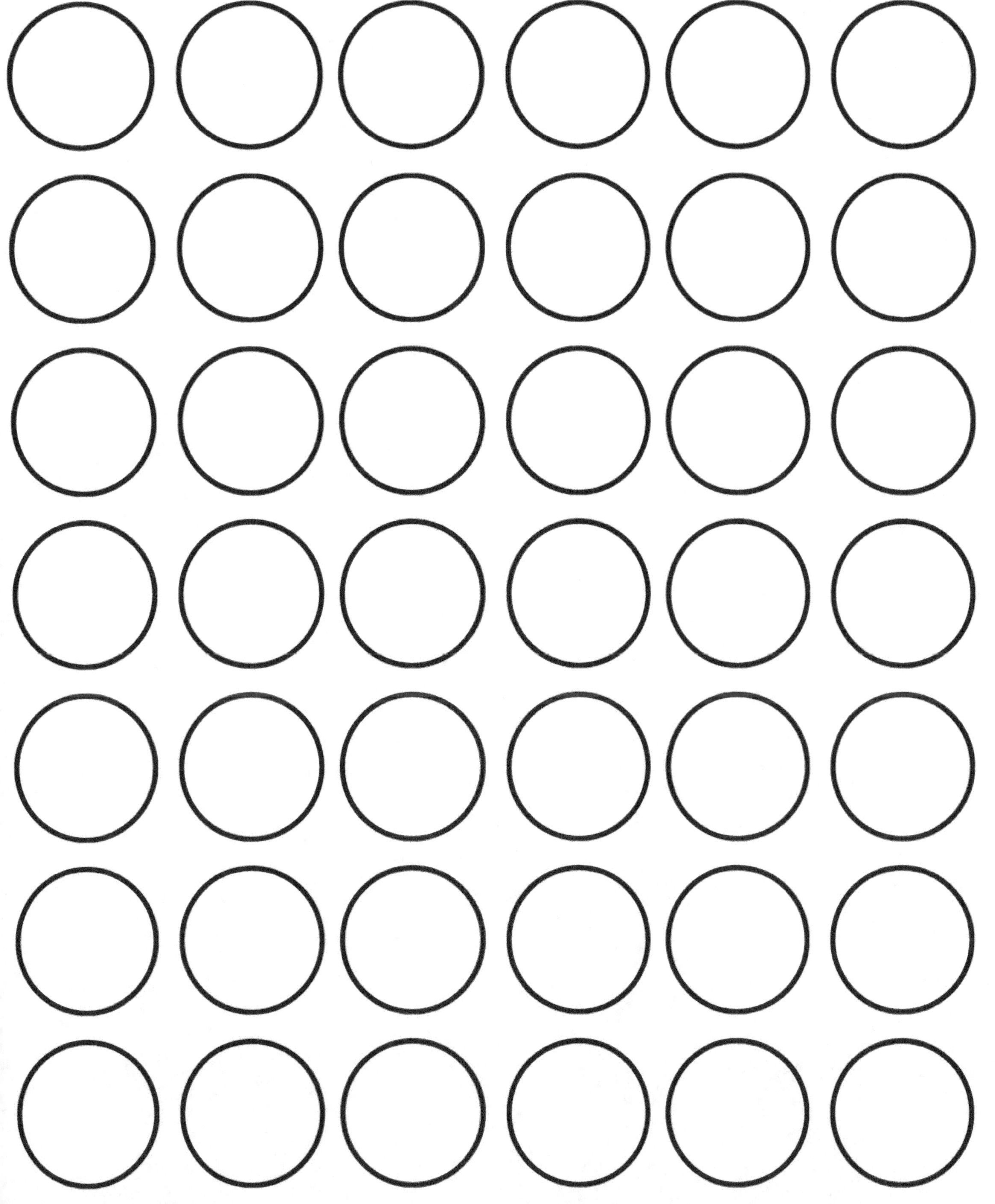

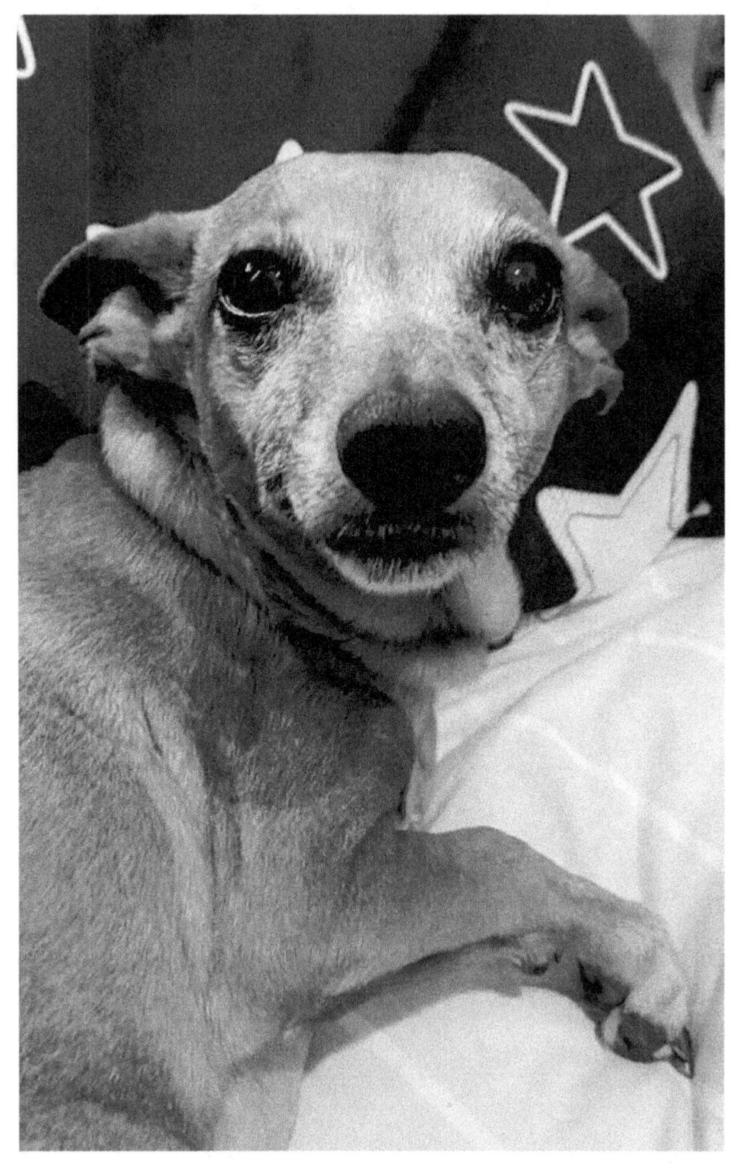

this book Is dedicated to Pinchi.
the goodest good boy there ever was.

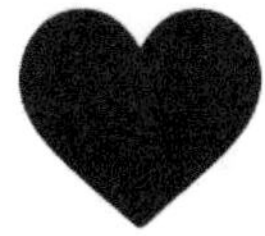